MagicImage Filmbooks
presents

THE MUMMY'S CURSE
(Including the Original Shooting Script)

by Gregory W. Mank

Introduction by Ron Chaney
Foreword by John Conforti

UNIVERSAL FILMSCRIPT SERIES
CLASSIC HORROR
Volume 11

THE MUMMY'S CURSE
(Including the Original Shooting Script)

FIRST EDITION

Published by MagicImage Filmbooks
740 S. Sixth Avenue
Absecon, NJ 08201
Phone: (609) 652-6500
Fax: (609) 748-9776
www.magicimage.com
sales@magicimage.com

Copyright ©2000, MagicImage Productions, Inc.
All Rights Reserved.

Reproduction in whole or in part is prohibited without the written permission of the copyright holder.

Photographs, filmscript and other production materials used with the permission of and by special arrangement with Universal Studios.

The film *THE MUMMY'S CURSE* copyright © 1944 by Universal Pictures Company, Inc. Renewed 1971 by Universal Pictures. All Rights Reserved.

MAGICIMAGE PRODUCTIONS, INC.

Publisher
Michael D. Stein

Managing Editor
John Conforti

Layout Assistant
Lauren Conforti

Administrative Assistant
Tracy Grosso

The purpose of this series is the preservation of the art of writing for the screen. Rare books have long been a source of enjoyment and an investment for the serious collector, and even in limited printings there usually were a few thousand produced. Scripts however, numbered only 50 at the most, and we are proud to present them in their original form. Some will be final shooting scripts and some earlier drafts, so that students, libraries, archives and film-lovers, archives, and film-lovers might, for the first time, study them in their original form. In producing these volumes, we hope that the unique art of screenplay writing will be preserved for future generations.

The opinions expressed in this book are those of the individual authors and not the publisher.

Special Thanks to Mr. Philip Riley

The Library of Congress Cataloging in Publication Data:

Mank, Gregory W.
  The mummy's curse : (including the original shooting script) / [Gregory W. Mank and John W. Conforti].-- 1st ed.
     p. cm.
  -- (Universal filmscripts series. Classic horror films ; v. 11)
     ISBN 1-882127-35-8 (alk. paper)
  1. Mummy's curse (Motion picture) I. Conforti, John W., 1966- II. Title. III. Series.
 PN1997.M817 M36 2000
 791.43'72--dc21

                          00-008722

  791.43'72--dc20   94-2398
                          CIP

**Manufactured in the
United States of America
Printed and Bound by
Data Reproductions Corp., Inc.**

Kharis (Chaney) carries princess Ananka (Virginia Christine) away to his temple

Preface
by John Conforti

THE CURSE OF THE MUMMY

Frankenstein, Dracula, and the Mummy--all three have two things in common: 1) each embodies a different aspect of our psychological fears of life after death and 2) each was, at some time, played by Lon Chaney, Jr.

Lon Chaney, Jr. had a remarkable career. For *The Mummy's Curse* he endured and suffered for a role, which, by all accounts, he did not even like! Karloff was in wraps for only one scene in the original film. Chaney had to endure weeks in the sweltering heat of southern California under head to toe bandaging and layer upon layer of heavy make up without hardly time for a break. The production pace of a "B" movie allows no rest for the weary.

The flashing glance at his life and career we gain in this volume once again teases us to see the completion of the long awaited *Century of Chaneys* volumes. Someday, all the slices of life **MagicImage** and others have published over the years will become part of a whole, the pieces in order, all the gaps filled in.

The bandaged, perambulating monstrosity Chaney played in *The Mummy's Curse* has long intrigued me. What can possibly be threatening about a slowly shifting collection of beragged bones? Surely, even a man on crutches could outrun him. That is, provided he does not stop to marvel at the monstrosity.

Frankenstein's monster represents the new concepts of death conquered by science. He is strong and violent, filled with the unbridled, undisciplined passions of youth. We fear trapping the beauty of our humanity in the contorted contraptions produced by science and technology....a clumsy, stitched together, bastardized copy of God's wondrous creation.

Dracula represents death conquered by medieval magic embodying the aristocratic concept of entitlement. Possessed of superior powers and wealth, he is free to roam, sucking the blood of the peasants to maintain his existence. Age has taught him patience. His sinister evil is amplified by his quiet resolve to have all he desires. The vampire is calm, refined, sexually alluring in the confidence and power he exudes. We fear him because he is all we dare not be....ruthless, bloodthirsty, without conscience. We fear becoming him as much as we long to be him; we fear being his victim as much as we long to be in his arms.

The Mummy has them both beat by eons. He is unbelievably ancient...stretching back to the very beginnings of human culture. His is a death conquered in the mysterious times of humanity's birth. He evokes not only the awesome wonders of ancient Egypt, but of

all our societies' origins concealed by the misty veil of time measured in millennia. His shuffling decrepitness conjures images of Druids making human sacrifice; of human blood running down the steps of Aztec temples; rites and rituals so ancient and fearful on the visceral level that we would seek to deny our tie to the roots in the bloody soil in which the Mummy was buried. That is until one watches the nightly news...dead soldiers dragged through streets, dead children found in garbage cans. Stripped of its ritual and meaning, man's brutality remains, as a bandaged monstrosity at our backs, tenacious, relentless, always threatening to overtake us. Bereft of mind, heart, and soul, it menaces us from the shadows of our collective unconscious.

And yet we stop to marvel at his longevity...and desire to understand his secret. Even deeper in our psyche however, we know what it would mean to live with the Mummy's Curse......to live forever....so long in a world that, at its core, is as unchanging and tenacious as the Mummy himself. So many of us waste the 60, 70, 80 years we have. What more would we do with 10,000? Thus the decrepit immortality of the Mummy forces us to accept our own mortality. His is a curse; ours is freedom, for only in the acceptance that our time is short can we seek the urgency for change.

And so, Kharis trails behind us, shuffling in the dark shadow we cast, always a few steps out of reach. And the only way he can catch us is if we stop too long to marvel.

John Conforti
January 14, 2000

Introduction
by Ron Chaney

Believe it or not, Lon Chaney Jr's. role as Kharis in *The Mummy's Curse* was not one of his personal favorites, even though it solidified him as Universal's top horror film star of the 1940s. While he was most grateful for that fact, the role itself was less than desirable. My grandfather stated in several interviews, that the makeup took hours to apply and was very hot and uncomfortable. In addition to the grueling procedure of applying the makeup, the role did not allow for any speaking parts. I know this must have bothered him, just as it would any other actor. But despite the restrictions of makeup and lack of dialog, gramps was able to stamp Kharis with his own unique touch by developing the Mummy's familiar gait, dragging one leg and extending one arm. His imposing size and strength also added to the character and even with only one eye visible through the makeup, he managed to emote fear, anger, and sympathy.

I have been told by many fans, that of all the roles my grandfather portrayed, this one in particular generated more fear and sleepless nights than any other role. Was it his interpretation of Kharis? his makeup? the atmosphere? or perhaps it was the anticipation of the unexpected that created this response. Regardless of what element caused these reactions, this film has given many hours of entertainment to multiple generations.

A temporal anachronism...ancient Mummy (Chaney) meets modern technology.

Gramps portrayed Kharis in three films: *The Mummy's Tomb*, *The Mummy's Ghost*, and *The Mummy's Curse* leaving an indelible impression on the American public as to the look of a living mummy. His portrayal as the mute Kharis the Mummy, the tortured Lawrence Talbot in *The Wolf Man*, the ferocity and tenderness embodied in the Frankenstein's Monster in *The Ghost of Frankenstein*, and the cold evil of Count Alucard in *Son of Dracula*, demonstrated his versatility and earned him the title "The Screen's Master Character Creator." This distinction set him apart from other horror actors and contributed to his drawing power at the box office and popularity with the public.

I am very proud of my grandfather's diversity in character portrayals and his contribution to the field of the performing arts. He made even rough hewn parts like Kharis shine like gems. This scriptbook by *MagicImage* shall fit nicely into the collections of all classic horror film fans including my own. So brew some tanna leaf tea, start *The Mummy's Curse* on video, follow the script and enjoy the show.

Sincerely,

Ron Chaney
Chaney Entertainment, Inc.

Ron Chaney (right) and MagicImage Managing Editor John Conforti.

THE MUMMY'S CURSE

Production History
by
Gregory Wm. Mank

"The Mummy's on the loose and he's dancing with the Devil!"

- *The Mummy's Curse*, 1944

A SWAMP on Universal's back lot - August, 1944.

Suddenly, a hand rises out of the mud, grasping toward the rejuvenating sun. The quagmire quivers and there arises a female mummy, horrifically caked with muck, stretching, jerking and falling as she escapes the boggy grave. Feminine vanity prevails, and the lady mummy makes for a pool to bathe away her full-length mudpack. Glamorously she emerges - in sexy black wig, clinging white nightgown and 1944 false eyelashes, as the reincarnation of Egypt's "Princess Ananka."

Thusly did actress Virginia Christine go on to vamp Lon Chaney's Kharis the Mummy and give one of the most dynamic performances of Universal's long-celebrated horror shows in *The Mummy's Curse*, fourth of the studio's ever-popular sequels to 1932's *The Mummy*.

In Universal's classic *The Mummy* (1932), a fiery bolt from Isis had zapped Karloff, reducing the star bogeyman to a pile of dry bones, his cracked skull grinning forlornly under his fez in the fadeout.

Of course, Universal never could resist resurrecting its prize hobgoblins. And, by 1944, the shooting of a *Mummy* sequel on the back lot had become almost a traditional Summer event - like some macabre picnic with an Egyptian motif.

The sequels had begun in the summer of 1940, as Universal shot *The Mummy's Hand*. Saturday matinee cowboy star Tom Tyler (himself doomed by the curse of arthritis) played the 3700-year old Kharis. Peggy Moran was the heroine in negligee, Dick Foran and Wallace Ford the wise-cracking archaeologist heroes, and George Zucco played the wonderfully wicked high priest who revitalized the Mummy with Tana leaves under the full moon. Christy Cabanne directed.

Virginia Christine, in a dazzling bit of Hollywood black magic, emerges from the swamp as the mud-caked mummy Princess Ananka

By the end of the picture, Zucco's high priest had been shot, and tumbled down the temple steps; Tyler's Mummy burned alive. *The Mummy's Hand* opened at New York City's Rialto Theatre in September of 1940.

The Mummy's Hand became one of Universal's two biggest moneymaking "B" films of the year (the other being the comedy *Oh, Johnny, How You Can Love.*) And as happens in Hollywood when a sequel makes money, another was shortly in the works.

Come the Summer of 1942, and Universal was shooting *The Mummy's Tomb*. "The fire that sought to consume Kharis," rasped Zucco (having miraculously survived the bullets and temple stairs fall from *The Mummy's Hand*, and epically aged), "only seared and twisted and maimed." Inheriting the role of Kharis was Lon Chaney, Jr. fresh from *The Wolf Man* and *The Ghost of Frankenstein*, billed by Universal as "The Screen's Master Character Creator." Limping on his one good leg, strangling with his one good arm, and rolling his one good eye, Chaney's Kharis invades New England, dispatched by the ancient Zucco, tended by hot-blooded young high priest Turhan Bey; Kharis manages to kill *The Mummy's Hand* survivors Foran and Ford before Bey's lust for heroine Elyse Knox upsets the holy mission.

This time, the final reel finds Miss Knox in the traditional nightgown, the Mummy carrying her about a fiery New England mansion, the torch-bearing villagers (augmented by footage from the climax of *Frankenstein*) roasting Kharis. Harold Young directed. The film was a smash hit, breaking records at the NY Rialto Theatre, where it was the Halloween, 1942 attraction.

Summer, 1943: Universal's back lot hosted Chaney's Kharis once more in *The Mummy's Ghost*. Zucco (more trembling, palsied and fanatical than ever) sends great Shakespearean actor/Hollywood villain John Carradine to find Kharis in the New England countryside. He then sets up quarters with him on a wonderfully picturesque old mining shack high atop a mining trestle and invokes the full moon-wrath of Amon-Ra. The heroine is Ramsay Ames, embellished with a wonderfully dramatic touch of two silver streaks shooting through her brunette hair whenever the Mummy crosses her path. Come the climax, Carradine, too, succumbs to the joys of the flesh, coveting Miss Ames and offering her the time-honored wedding gift of eternal life. Chaney's Mummy knocks him out of the mining shack window, lugs Miss Ames (nightgowned, naturally, and rapidly aging a la *Lost Horizon*) into the New England swampland where both sink before the awed eyes of the ever-torch-bearing villagers.

Reginald Le Borg directed. *The Mummy's Ghost* arrived at New York's Rialto in time for the 4th of July, 1944 holiday. The fans of melodrama still lined up, although the critics had long been gunning for Universal's Mummy. Alton Cook of the *New York World Telegram* reported: "The Mummy always has been the least impressive of movie monsters and he is doing nothing to enhance his reputation in his latest incarnation in *The Mummy's Ghost*...he is just repulsive without being picturesque or even particularly frightening."

Despite critical attacks, Universal's Mummy series found its loyal audience. That these little, 60-minute sequels could never contest the beauty and romanticism of the original *The Mummy*, starring Karloff and Zita Johann, directed by Karl Freund, was hardly important. The Universal sequels had a folklore all their own. There was something wonderfully spooky about Kharis, sipping his Tana leaves, shuffling across Universal's back lot under the full moon, performing his weird, shuffling dance to the strains of Hans J. Salter's rhapsodic music.

Nevertheless, by 1944, the *Mummy* series had become predictable, almost as ritualistic as a traditional religious rite with its torch-bearing villagers, lustful high priests, and, of course, nightgowned heroines. If Chaney's Kharis was to rise once more, the film would need novelty.

And novelty is just what it got.

Universal blueprinted *The Mummy's Return* (as it was originally titled) as part of its 1944/1945 horror program. On May 8, 1944, the studio had completed its "spectacular" for the season - *House Of Frankenstein* , featuring Mad Doctor Karloff, Hunchback J. Carrol Naish, Lon Chaney as the Wolf Man, John Carradine as Count Dracula, Glenn Strange as Frankenstein's Monster, Elena Verdugo as the Gypsy Girl, Anne Gwynne, Lionel Atwill, George Zucco...

Virginia Christine tends to Chaney's Mummy on Universal's back lot.

Resurrected in Horror! Rising out of Death! Egypt's Ancient Lovers...Live again in Evil...to fulfill...*The Mummy's Curse*.

- from the preview trailer for
The Mummy's Curse

"Man, Oh , Man!" crowed Universal's trade advertisement for *House Of Frankenstein*. "This show's gonna scare the yell out of Satan himself!"

Perhaps the fact that Kharis was left out of this monster rally prompted a new Mummy vehicle. Universal was taking stock: after all, Karloff had completed his 2-picture star contract (*The Climax*, with Susanna Foster, and *House Of Frankenstein*), and, in May of 1944, had joined Val Lewton's RKO Horror Unit, where he'd star in *The Body Snatcher, Isle Of The Dead* and *Bedlam*. Universal's "Scream Queen" Evelyn Ankers, fresh from her perils in the clutches of the Wolf Man, Frankenstein Monster, Mad Ghoul, Dracula, Paula the Ape Woman and the Invisible Man (indeed, every studio monster BUT the Mummy!), wrapped up her contract that summer in *The Frozen Ghost* (with Chaney), and left for Malibu to await the birth of her daughter.

Miss Ankers had long tired of the wicked pace of her Universal melodramas and the scream she so lushly sounded in them. "It was always nerve-wracking and a tremendous effort for me," said the actress (who died in Hawaii in 1985).

Producer Oliver Drake goes over the melody of "Monsieur Legood-for Nothing" which he composed for the film, with Ann Codee, former French musical hall artist.

Acquanetta, who enjoyed a little notoriety as Ape Woman Paula in *Captive Wild Woman* and *Jungle Woman*, also left the lot. When Universal began a third "Paula the Ape Woman" saga, *The Jungle Captive*, Vicky Lane inherited the Paula hair and fangs. Acquanetta, tiring of the "B" histrionics, had departed Universal for Monogram (which was hardly a step up!).

Lon Chaney, however, was still a major Universal attraction. He'd already played the Wolf Man in the spring of 1944 in *House of Frankenstein*, so Universal decided to keep him busy in a new Mummy movie - hence the fourth Mummy sequel, *The Mummy's Curse* which perpetuated the saga of the lovelorn Kharis.

Once again, it was a summer event. Ben Pivar, who had produced all of Universal's *Mummy* sequels, again headed up operations on this new film. Oliver Drake, best-remembered for his western work (and a close friend of Chaney), was Associate Producer. Bernard L. Schubert wrote the screenplay and contributed to the original story, taking home the largest paycheck of the four writers ($1833.36) who contributed: Leon Abrams ($1000), T. H. Richmond ($550) and Dwight V. Babcock ($433.34).

This task force of writers developed the fresh gimmick: Princess Ananka, carried beneath the swamp by Kharis, would rise from the bog, in full view of the audience - then become a sexy young woman to vitalize the sensational tone of the melodrama.

Although Universal's horror series usually relied on certain inconsistencies to pave the way from sequel to sequel, *The Mummy's Curse* asked special indulgence from its audiences. Swallowed up in a New England swamp in *The Mummy's Ghost*, Kharis and Ananka turn up in *The Mummy's Curse* in the bayou of Louisiana with the script dialogue insisting this was where the last film was set. Also, supposedly 25 years have passed - making the time period of the new film 1969!

The Mummy's Curse fell quickly into place, with a $123,000 budget, a 12-day shooting schedule - and a very professional cast.

THE PLAYERS

For what was to be the final Mummy sequel, Universal had assembled a dynamic group of players. It was a mix of old-line contract players, some relegated from stardom to the "B" circuit, and fresh, up and coming talent cutting teeth on the same circuit.

THE MUMMY: For the third (and final) time, Lon Chaney would play Kharis. The boisterous Universal star had not been too discreet in letting everyone know just how little he cared for playing this monstrous, one-eyed ragbag.

"I sweat and I can't wipe it away," Chaney had bemoaned on the set of *The Mummy's Ghost*. "I itch and I can't scratch!"

Still, it was a lucrative job. His Universal salary had escalated since he made his debut there in *Man Made Monster* (1941). The 38-year old star would earn $8000 for the 2 weeks he labored on THE MUMMY'S CURSE.

Lon Chaney, Jr. As Kharis, The Mummy

PAYROLL
THE MUMMY'S CURSE

Lon Chaney, Jr. - *Kharis, The Mummy*	$ 8,000.00
Peter Coe, *Dr. Ilzor Zandaab*	$ 3,500.00
Leslie Goodwins, Director	$ 2,500.00
Bernard L. Schubert, Writer	$ 1,833.36
Oliver Drake, Producer	$ 1,500.00
Martin Kosleck, *Ragheb*	$ 1,200.00
Dennis Moore, *Dr. James Halsey*	$ 1,000.00
Ben Pivar, Executive Producer	$ 1,000.00
Leon Abrams, Writer	$ 1,000.00
Kay Harding, *Betty Walsh*	$ 750.00
Kurt Katch, *Cajun Joe*	$ 750.00
Addison Richards, *Pat Walsh*	$ 700.00
Napoleon Simpson, *Goobie*	$ 750.00
Holmes Herbert, *Dr. Cooper*	$ 600.00
Virginia Christine, *Princess Ananka*	$ 541.67
William Farnum, *The Sacristan*	$ 150.00

DR. ILZOR ZANDAAB: The latest evil Egyptian high priest to tend to Kharis was played by Peter Coe, a Yugoslavian-born actor who had come to Universal by way of London's Royal Academy of Dramatic Art. He had taken the post of Johnny Weissmuller's understudy in Billy Rose's *Aquacade*, and had acted in a number of Broadway plays. Coe had co-starred with Maria Montez and Jon Hall in Universal's *Gypsy Wildcat* and had played Anne Gwynne's husband in *House Of Frankenstein*. He later played in such films as *Sands Of Iwo Jima, Can-Can* and *Snow White Meets The Three Stooges*. He was also the personal choice of the notorious Edward D. Wood, Jr. to play Bela Lugosi in the Bela biopic Wood never managed to make. Peter Coe died in Los Angeles in 1993.

Coe landed the second-largest salary on *The Mummy's Curse*: a flat fee of $3500.

Kay Harding's parents, Mr. And Mrs. J.H. Harding, moved to Hollywood to make a home for her. She had been living at the Hollywood Studio Club for girls since her husband, L.N. Patterson, joined the Navy to fight in World War II.

"Maybe this will start a new fad in women's hats," comments Peter Coe, placing his Egyptian fez on Kay Harding.

BETTY WALSH - the role of the spirited heroine went to Universal contractee Kay Harding, who also acted in such Universal films of the era as the Sherlock Holmes thrillers *The Scarlet Claw (1944)* and *The Woman In Green* (1945). For *The Mummy's Curse*, Kay Harding received the flat fee of $750.

DR. JAMES HALSEY-Filling the shoes of the proverbial archaeologist hero was Dennis Moore, who had just wrapped up a major role in Universal's serial *Raiders Of Ghost City* (1944). He had a curious career: playing everything from the villain of the Bowery Boys *Spooks Run Wild* (Monogram, 1941, with Lugosi as the red herring) to starring in such serials as *The Purple Monster Strikes* and *The Master Key*. Dennis Moore continued his work in serials and starred in the last two serials ever produced: *Blazing The Overland Trail* and *Perils Of The Wilderness*. He died in 1964, at the age of 56. Dennis Moore signed for 2 weeks' work on THE MUMMY'S CURSE at $500 per week - total, $1000.

Dialogue director Lewis Norman (with script) coaches players in the Cajun dialect of Louisiana's Bayou country. Players are (from left to right) Peter Coe, Holmes Herbert, Dennis Moore and Virginia Christine.

RAGHEB: No MUMMY film was complete without the lustful acolyte of Amon-Ra; Universal was fortunate in signing Martin Kosleck, the dark, diminutive Hollywood heavy who was known for his Goebbels impersonations, to follow in the wicked ways of George Zucco, Turhan Bey and John Carradine. As David Ragan wrote in WHO'S WHO OF HOLLLYWOOD, 1900 - 1976: "With his high cheekbones, Teutonic accent and wickedly slanted eyes, not to mention his icy - hearted demeanor, he was the nastiest movie 'Nazi' of them all. For years, in the '40s, he had audiences spitting venom at the screen." He acted on Broadway and radio, and was an accomplished painter. Bette Davis and Marlene Dietrich owned some of his work. His most indelible horror role was undoubtedly the mad sculptor of Universal's *House of Horrors* (1946) who uses the Creeper (Rondo Hatton) to kill his critics. After a final decade of serious illness, Martin Kosleck died in 1994. Martin Kosleck signed for $800 per week, with a week-and-a-half commitment: total, $1200.

The rest of the cast joined up: Kurt Katch (1896 - 1958, whose scene as a Gypsy whose bear fights Chaney's Larry Talbot in *The Wolfman* had been cut), played Cajun Joe, the lusty laborer killed by the Mummy - one week's work at $750. Addison Richards (c. 1887 - 1964) played Pat Walsh, the

Peter Coe (left) and Martin Kosleck flank Lon Chaney as he sips the magic Tana leaf brew.

construction boss and heroine's uncle - Seven days' work for a total of $700; black actor Napoleon Simpson played the laborer Goobie, for $750. A last-minute addition to the cast was Holmes Herbert (1882-1956), the British actor who had played in such horror classics as Paramount's *Dr. Jekyll and Mr. Hyde* (1931), Warners' *Mystery of the Wax Museum* (1933), MGM's *Mark of the Vampire* (1935) - as well as such Universal titles as *The Ghost of Frankenstein* (1942), *Invisible Agent* (1942), and a number of Sherlock Holmes thrillers. Herbert's salary: $600.

However, still the role that demanded (and promised) most - was Ananka. Universal selected a promising blonde actress, who had starred on the Los Angeles stage as HEDDA GABLER (1942), played impressively in Warner Bros.' *Edge of Darkness* (1943, starring Errol Flynn), and had just teamed diabolically with Lionel Atwill in Universal's serial *Raiders of Ghost City* (1944).

Lon Chaney & Kurt Katch

Her name - Virginia Christine.

For many years, Virginia Christine (who died in 1996) and her husband, super character actor Fritz Feld (who died in 1993), were among the best-loved actors of the movie colony. They lived in an ocean-view house in Brentwood, west of Hollywood, and it was there that Ms. Christine remembered the real-life horrors of *The Mummy's Curse*.

Lon Chaney, director Leslie Goodwins and Virginia Christine relax in the summer heat during the shooting of The Mummy's Curse.

Brentwood, CA, 1987; Author Greg Mank visits Virginia and her husband Fritz Feld at their ocean-view home.

"Before I could be OK'd for the part, I had to go see Jack Pierce, the head of the makeup department, and he had to look at the contours of my face to see if he could make a mummy out of me. Jack was a big braggadocio - he did create all the Frankensteins, and was a master of the monster pictures - and he wanted the news to go around that he was about to do something new."

Pierce approved; Virginia Christine signed to play Ananka in *The Mummy's Curse*, for $250 per week, and for 2 weeks and a day - total, $541.67.

THE DIRECTOR

London-born Leslie Goodwins had a reputation in Hollywood for speed, efficiency and good humor. For RKO he had directed two-dozen films, including seven of the *Mexican Spitfire* series, with Lupe Velez. By 1944, he was running back and forth between RKO and Universal, where he had directed 1944's *The Singing Sheriff*, *Hi Beautiful* and *Murder in the Blue Room* before taking over *The Mummy's Curse*.

Goodwins later directed such films as *Genius at Work* (RKO, 1946), which pitted the comedy team of Wally Brown and Alan Carney against Bela Lugosi and Lionel Atwill; *Dragnet* (Screen Guild, 1947); *Fireman, Save My Child* (1954), a Universal-International project abandoned by Abbott and Costello (Hugh O'Brian and Buddy Hackett replaced Bud and Lou); and Allied Artists' *Paris Follies of 1956*. His final credit: *Tammy and the Millionaire* (Universal, 1967), which he co-directed with Sidney Miller and Ezra Stone. Leslie Goodwins died January 8, 1970.

Universal engaged "Les" Goodwins for four weeks' work on *The Mummy's Curse* including preparation and wrap-up time, at $625 per week. Total: $2500.

PRODUCTION NOTES

Thanks to the sets standing on Universal's wonderfully picturesque back lot, *The Mummy's Curse* was able to visit various locales which, with a bit of set dressing, served perfectly The lower level of the *Tower of London* (1939) set would provide the interior of the monastery ceremonial room, cell and side room (with a modest $2100 revamping); the jungle from *Gung Ho!* (1943) would serve as the exterior of the construction camp (with $2815 worth of adjustments); the exterior monastery steps, courtesy of James Whale's *Green Hell* (1940), decorated the hillside of Pollard Lake, with a $575 makeover. And $400 (down from the originally estimated $500!) was all that was needed to transform Universal's "Singapore Street" set into the exterior of Tante Berthe's cafe, and rear entrance.

Universal budgeted the "Trick, Miniatures & Process" estimate, including "Special Tricks - Breakaways Tents and Operations" at a mere $2650.

Total wardrobe expense was estimated at only $2400 - with Virginia Christine and Kay Harding in a tie for best-accoutered cast member, each with $400 worth of costumes. The cost for Chaney's Mummy costume - $100.

Music had played a part in recent Universal horror shows - the "Faro La, Faro Li" festival number from *Frankenstein Meets the Wolfman* (1943), and Elena Verdugo's Gypsy dance in *House of Frankenstein* - - Universal estimated $2900, to shoot the song numbers at Tante Berthe's Cajun casino. For the swamp exteriors, the studio rented a steam shovel for one day ($250), a bulldozer for three days ($50 per day), and four trucks for three days (at $25 per day each.) There was the $1650 "Make-up and Hairdressing Estimate," which included the services of the makeup staff and "Allowance for wigs - masks - clay, etc." Joe Hadley was official makeup supervisor on the film, although Jack Pierce, of course, would mastermind the Mummy makeups.

Finally, production was ready to go. Of course, the censors were ever-vigilant. On July 21, 1944, Joseph I. Breen wrote this letter of warning to Universal:

"...Ananka, the Egyptian girl, is described in several places as 'rather lightly clothed in a nightgown.' It will be absolutely essential to see that she is properly clothed in such a way as not to expose her body, and when the clothes are described as 'wet,' they should not offensively outline her body. Likewise, we urge upon you the necessity of avoiding any undue gruesomeness in the scenes where the various people are killed..."

Princess Ananka (Virginia Christine) is slowly restored to youth by the sun's rays.

The real "gruesomeness," meanwhile, was in Jack P. Pierce's makeup laboratory. Virginia Christine never knew that Jack Pierce was experimenting with a magnificent makeup for her Female Mummy - so magnificent, in fact, that it ran the risk of scarring this beautiful actress for life.

Mercifully unaware, Virginia Christine reported for shooting of *The Mummy's Curse*.

"I loved myself in that black wig. I thought I was smashing!"

- *Virginia Christine*

8:30 a.m., Wednesday, July 26, 1944: *The Mummy's Curse* began shooting, with Dennis Moore, Kay Harding, Virginia Christine and Peter Coe all starting work that day. The company worked on the "Int. Halsey's tent" set on Soundstage 17, then moved to the back lot and "Lubin Lake" for "Ext. Halsey's Tent & Camp" shooting. The summer heat was sadistic, with planes flying overhead spoiling several takes. Still, Goodwins wrapped up work at 5:55 p.m., having shot 13 camera set-ups.

Come day two, and there was trouble. Peter Coe and Martin Kosleck reported at 8:30 a.m. to the Int. Monastery set, in the old "Tower of London." At nine o'clock, William Farnum joined them. Once a major silent screen star (he fought Tom Santschi in the 1914 version of *The Spoilers*, as well as being prominent in such silents as *A Tale of Two Cities*, *If I Were King* and *Les Miserables*), he also was the brother of silent cowboy star Dustin Farnum, who had died in 1929. The 67-year old Farnum had signed a "Day Player Agreement" to play the bit role of the Sacristan in *The Mummy's Curse*. His fee for the film: $150. It was clearly a drop from his days of Silent Screen stardom.

When Chaney first appeared on the set in Mummy regalia at noon on July 27, he found a sad sight: Farnum, old and nervous, could not get out his few lines. And director Goodwins was becoming impatient.

Lon Chaney & William Farnum

"This man was a friend of my dad's," Peter Coe recalled Chaney saying. "He was a big star!"

At which time Chaney stormed into the production office, demanded "a star chair for Mr. Farnum with his name on it" and that he be treated "with the respect that he deserves!" -otherwise Chaney would not go back to work. While the sight of Universal's "Mummy" laying down the law to the front office paints a comic picture, it was successful: Farnum got his chair and respect - and Goodwins got the sequence in the can that evening by 6:55 p.m.

The shooting went on in the terrific heat. All the stars were on call Friday, July 28, as well as 24 extras. There were stand-ins, too. Robert Pepper became Chaney's Mummy double, earning $35 each day he reported to the set.

Despite the double, the shooting of *The Mummy's Curse* wore on Chaney. Although the shooting schedule allowed the star to report to the set his first two days at mid-day, his designated arrival time soon changed to 10 a.m., to 9 a.m., to 8:30 a.m.; he often spent 10-hour days in the torturous Kharis get-up. As he told CASTLE OF FRANKENSTEIN magazine (#10, 1966):

"In those three pictures, I was completely covered from head to foot with a suit and rubber mask; the only thing that was exposed was my eye! In the last of that series, the temperature was in the upper nineties. It was so hot that I went to my dressing room between scenes, opened a refrigerator and lay down next to it. It was my only relief from the heat..."

Tragically, Lon Chaney had a thirst for more than just Tana leaves. As Virginia Christine recalls:

"Evelyn Ankers had played Lon Chaney's leading lady, and she was a big girl, a heavy girl. So Chaney had asked that they design a strap that went around his neck and around her waist to take some of the weight off his arms.

"One day on the back lot, we were doing this shot in which the Mummy was to carry me up to the old shrine, the monastery, up these steep, crooked, worn steps. They were hard enough to navigate if you were

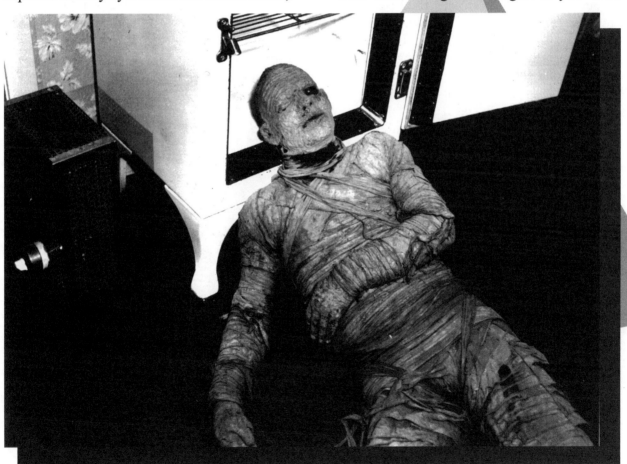

Lon Chaney tries to cool down from the sadistic California heat in his dressing room.

sober. And there I was, with this strap inherited from Evelyn Ankers attached to my waist, around Lon Chaney's neck, starting up these steps - and he is absolutely stoned. I always hate, when they're gone, to say bad things, but it was an actual fact - Chaney was just stoned. He was pretty much throughout the picture. We start up the steps, and he's WEAVING, going side-to-side on these uneven steps! Chaney was a big guy, and if he fell down those stone steps, with me attached to him, I hate to think what would have happened!

"Finally, the director said, 'Cut!' and they took Chaney out of the Mummy suit, and put the stand-in into it. SO he carried me up - and I was enormously relieved!"

One especially grueling day on *The Mummy's Curse* was Thursday, August 3, 1944. Shooting began at 8:30 a.m. on the *Tower of London* exterior set (that served as the excavation sight) and continued through the day and into the night on Universal's "Singapore Street" (here doubling as Tante Berthe's cafe) and the *Gung Ho!* set (which featured the exterior shots of Betty's tent). By the time work ended at 10:15 that night, Chaney had put in a 12-hour day (with 2 hours off for meals) as the Mummy, coping with the heavy mask and costume and the sweltering California heat.

Dennis Moore and Martin Kosleck finished their work at 6:00 p.m. on Monday, August 7, on Universal's upper lake - here standing in as the Louisiana bayou swamps. On Tuesday, August 8, Ann Codee reported to Stage 16 to play Tante Berthe, the singing casino owner (she had pre-recorded her song "Hey You" on August 5, composed by Frank Orth and Oliver Drake , who was *The Mummy's Curse* associate producer. Drake also composed "Monsieur Le Good for Nothin," for this film, and licensed both songs to Universal - for $1.00 each! By 7:17 that night, she had filmed her entire role - dialogue, song, and being strangled to death by the Mummy! She did it all in one remarkable day's work.

The Mummy (Chaney) attacks Cajun Joe (Kurt Katch)

On August 9, Kay Harding, Kurt Katch and Holmes Herbert all finished their scenes - the fast-shooting Goodwins worked the company until 11:05pm. However, on the last day of shooting, August 10, 1944, Goodwins outdid himself. In one unbelievable day's shooting, Goodwins did 26 camera set-ups! Some were in the Exterior Jungles and Swamp. Others, such as the interior of Walsh's office, were on the "Phantom stage,"

Chaney's Mummy creeps up on Tante Berth (Ann Codee) as Ananka (Virginia Christine) watches in horror.

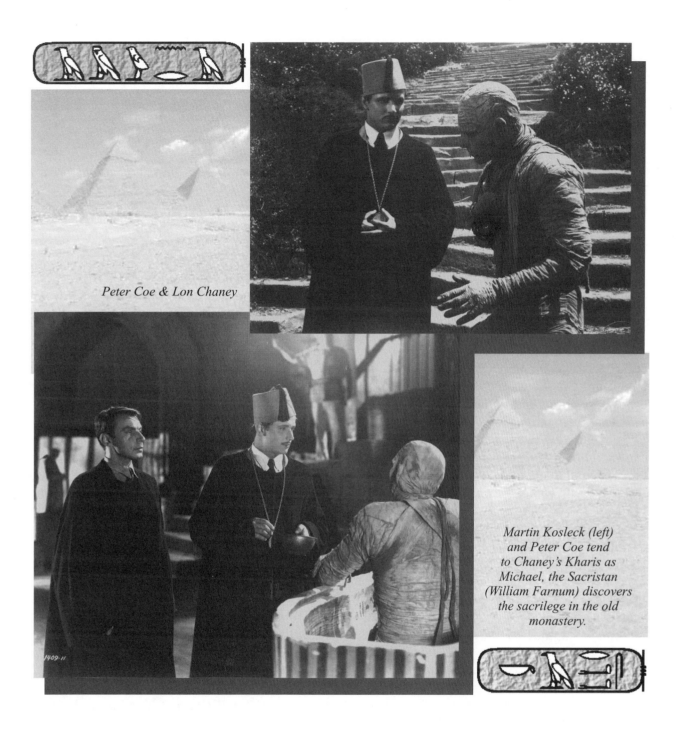

Peter Coe & Lon Chaney

Martin Kosleck (left) and Peter Coe tend to Chaney's Kharis as Michael, the Sacristan (William Farnum) discovers the sacrilege in the old monastery.

(so named for the Paris Opera House set built inside for Lon Chaney Sr.'s 1925 *The Phantom of theOpera* and refurbished for Universal's 1943 Technicolor version, with Claude Rains).

Virginia Christine finished that afternoon at 3:50. Dennis Moore, recalled for last-minute shooting, was done at 6:30. Peter Coe completed his role at 7:15.

The film was basically finished, only two days over schedule. The last player to lumber off the set of *The Mummy's Curse*, at 7:45 that night - Lon Chaney.

END OF PICTURE

That was the notation in Kenny's Assistant Director's Daily Report of August 10, 1944. However, there was a note: 32 scenes had not been shot, including the resurrection of the female mummy, Ananka.

"The vultures will pick the flesh from your bones after Kharis learns of your treachery!"

- Peter Coe, as the High Priest
in *The Mummy's Curse.*

Universal history was bizarrely repeating itself. In the original *The Mummy*, in 1932, a flashback episode, showing Zita Johann as "Anck-es-en-Amon" in her past lives (and later cut from the release print), had included a vignette with Zita as a Christian martyr - to be devoured by lions. According to Miss Johann (who died in 1993), Universal saved that shot for her last day - so that, if any of the lions overacted, the rest of the film was safely in the can!

A similar situation had evolved on *The Mummy's Curse*. Jack Pierce had devised a hideous mummy makeup for the beautiful Virginia Christine. There was only one problem: the makeup had the chance of scarring her features for life. As a Universal memo of September 22, 1944 later confided:

"As originally planned these scenes were actually to be made with trick photography. However, after we discovered that the makeup and conditions under which Miss Christine would have to work were apt to cause serious results to her features, this plan was abandoned..."

So, at the proverbial 11th hour, Universal and Jack P. Pierce jettisoned this remarkable and dangerous makeup. Unfortunately, the details of Pierce's original makeup appear lost to the ages.

Finally, on Monday, August 21, 1944, Universal recalled Virginia Christine (who had not been privy to any of these debates regarding the future of her face), for the final shot.

It was a day the actress would never forget.

"So...they saved that rejuvenation shot for the last day of shooting, so in case they killed me off, everything would be in the can! And Jack kept saying all through the picture, 'Virginia, don't you worry about your skin at all in the female mummy makeup. I'm using something different - just don't you worry.'

" Well! By the time we came to the last day of shooting, I was a wreck, and my husband, Fritz Feld, called Jack Pierce at night, at home, and said, 'Jack! PLEASE! Tell me what it is you're going to do to Virginia tomorrow!' And Jack said, "Tell her not to worry. It's just a 'Denver mudpack'."

The formidable "Denver mudpack" was obviously the replacement for the more elaborate (and destructive) makeup Pierce originally had designed. As it was, the new makeup was plenty gruesome for audiences- and for Virginia:

"I'll tell you how they did it. I was in the makeup chair, I think, at 4:30 in the morning. They took little patches of cotton, wet with witch hazel, put them on and lined them to fill in the youthful contours. Then Jack put on the 'Denver mudpack,' just a little bit at a time, then lined THAT with wrinkles then blow-dried it - each little patch until I was an absolutely rigid mask...And we made a mistake in wardrobe. We had the arms bare - so we had to do the arms and hands, too.

Below, Jack Pierce applies his makeup wizardry to turn Virginia Christine (left) into Ananka (below)

"Well, it took forever, and, of course, a very human thing happened - I had to go to the bathroom. Jack's wife was a body makeup lady, and she took me, like a child, to the bathroom, and pulled my panties down. Well, I have this sense of humor that's very close to the surface, but I couldn't laugh because the makeup would crack and they would have to start all over...It was just too ridiculous!"

Fortified by a malted milk, Miss Christine, in full mummy guise, was driven to the back lot. As Jack Pierce had hoped, word had spread about his new creation, and all of Universal (even Ingrid Bergman, who was visiting the lot that day) congregated to see the female mummy rise from its swampy grave:

"They took me out on the back lot, where the grave was dug, right in the soil - not clean, sifted sand! Then they covered me with burnt cork; then they sprayed it with water. Here I'm lying in the earth, with only my nostrils open for breathing - and I began to think of all the things that crawl in the earth...

"Then, at the last minute, they put the burnt cork (that looked like soil) over my face. I had to get up, and walk - into a stinking, slimy, infested pool, covered with algae, down two or three steps into the pond, and wade in up to my neck...

"Well, for the first time in my life, I was ready to scream, 'No, I can't do it!' because it's SO awful to look at! But then I thought, "You wanted to be an actress - let's go!

"Anyway, finally it was over, and then everybody was very helpful. The limousine was there, and they had a drink for me, and towels, and the whole bit."

A month after Virginia Christine's day in the swamp, Universal issued this memo to payroll:

#1409-Goodwins-THE MUMMY'S CURSE

"Kindly draw check in the amount of $250 to Miss Virginia Christine, which is in full settlement of her claim for intervening time between completion of her role in the above mentioned production and her recall for the photographing of trick shots..."

There were other curious aftermaths to *The Mummy's Curse*.

Universal took note of how much flashback footage from *The Mummy's Hand* (1940), featuring Tom Tyler as the Mummy, was showing up in *The Mummy's Curse* - hence this memo:

"We are entering into an agreement with TOM TYLER whereunder he releases to us, in consideration of the sum of $60, the use of certain film in which he appeared from MUMMY'S HAND. This film is to be used in our photoplay now entitled THE MUMMY'S CURSE.
"Will you therefore kindly draw a check in the amount of $60 payable to Mr. Tyler..."

Meanwhile, on September 15, ten singers had reported to Universal for *The Mummy's Curse* - eight men and two women - to sing the songs heard in the background of Tante Berthe's Café, each earning $20 for their labors.

All in all, *The Mummy's Curse* cost $127,535.61 - which was $4,535.61 over budget. The cost of Universal's classic *The Mummy* with Karloff in 1932, had been $196,000; the first sequel, 1940's *The Mummy's Hand*, had cost $84,000. So *The Mummy's Curse* cost was slightly less than the median between the tab of the 1932 original and the first sequel. It should be noted, however, that the final cost of *The Mummy's Curse* was about *one-third* of the minimum budget afforded a moderate Hollywood "A" release of the war years.

On December 22, 1944, The Hawaii Theatre in Hollywood offered a smash hit Horror premiere: Universal's *House of Frankenstein*, with *The Mummy's Curse* as the bottom half of a record-breaking double bill. Kharis made the rounds of the nation's key cities, accompanying *House of Frankenstein*, giving the double bill audiences the chance to see every Universal goblin save for Paula the Ape Woman and The Invisible Man.

However, the Rialto Theatre of New York City, the Horror showplace of America, rescued Kharis from the double bill and gave him a special honor: *The Mummy's Curse* would be the Easter attraction of the Rialto, opening at the 42nd street movie house March 30, 1945.

Of course, once settled into his popular, familiar surroundings, poor Kharis had to put up with his own menacing monsters...the Manhattan critics.

The New York WORLD-TELEGRAM:

"If the sweet idea of a visit from the Easter bunny happens to get on your nerves, you might drop over to the Rialto and watch Lon Chaney hobbling around again in his torn and dirty wrappings as the Mummy...Take a boresome neighbor whom you hope never will speak to you again.

This will do it."

The New York JOURNAL-AMERICAN:

"THE MUMMY'S CURSE, at the Rialto Theatre, finds Lon Chaney still galumphing around in a mudpack makeup, in search of the Princess Ananka...he drinks his magic brew of Tana leaves and scares everybody but the audience."

It was Archer Winsten, of the New York POST, who gave the most fair review in the Manhattan press:

" ...A thirteen-headed dragon could be no more preposterous, but people who gobble up this sort of thing are not students of possibilities.

"There is, though, one bit of fancy which has its own charm. Out of the mud track of a passing bulldozer you see a hand and then an arm emerge. Lo! It's a female mummy, the onetime girl of Chaney, somewhat the worse for dirt after all those years. She staggers off to the nearest pool, and when she comes out, she'd remind you of anything but a mummy. You will be safe in assuming that there has never been a mummy half as well built or a quarter as good-looking. Just for the record, her name is Virginia Christine.

"Lon Chaney pursues her, as who would not...."

The fans defied the critics; *The Mummy's Curse* was a hit. It also proved to be a very entertaining little melodrama, with much to recommend it.

Lon Chaney, once again, makes a formidable Kharis. In *The Mummy's Curse*, the actor had mastered the Mummy's quick, jerky, spasmodic movements in his violent scenes (which were many - he kills 5 characters onscreen in this 61 minute film!), and which contrast so well with the character's slow, shuffling gait. There's also the touch, in Chaney's *The Mummy's Curse* performance, of the melancholy, 3700-year old lover which Karloff had so beautifully conveyed in the original. One must wonder: WHAT would Universal Horror have done, during those World War II years, without Lon Chaney, Jr.?

Director Leslie Goodwins worked with Universal's technical departments to provide a slick atmosphere in *The Mummy's Curse*: the Louisiana bayou is a haunted place, with its torchlit canoes, rising mist and the moonlight that shimmers so eerily on the water. Camerman Virgil Miller makes the most of shadows, as when the Mummy strangles the Sacristan, and we see the action thrown up against the monastery wall, a shadow play, cleverly resembling a movie screen - a horror movie within a horror movie. And there's the effective little touch in Tante Berthe's death scene: as the woman fights the Mummy, beating against him, ancient dust arises from his battered body as he overpowers the woman.

The cast is convincing, and Martin Kosleck particularly villainous as the acolyte who, in Universal Mummy tradition, breaks his unholy vows for the joys of the flesh ("Master! I am but flesh and blood!").

However, the true star of THE MUMMY'S CURSE is Virginia Christine. The actress's resurrection scene is one of the most famous (and certainly one of the most frightening) episodes in all of Universal horror; the sight of this Sphinx-from-Hell, escaping her swampy grave, is the stuff great movie nightmares are made of. While the Jack P. Pierce "Denver Mudpack" is effective, it's Miss Christine's acting that really brings magic to this vignette, her pantomime fully conveying this unholy "thing" that has come back to life. And, as the glamorous Ananka, she also is impressive - sexy, dramatic, and fervently delivering lines like "He's coming for me...Kharis...Sometimes it seems as if I belong to a different world...!" as if Princess Ananka were one of the great roles of Classical Drama. The passion works - and wins Virginia Christine a special place on the Honor Roll of Universal Horror Performances.

THE MUMMY'S CURSE would be the final serious entry in Universal's MUMMY series. Universal did not find a place for Kharis in HOUSE OF DRACULA, shot in the early Fall of 1945, which did include Dracula (John Carradine), the Wolf Man (Chaney), Frankenstein's Monster (Glenn Strange) - as well as a hunchbacked nurse (Jane Adams) and Jekyll/Hyde scientist (Onslow Stevens). Chaney left the lot by 1946, as did most of the Universal attractions of the War Years (save for Deanna Durbin, Abbott & Costello, and a few others), when the studio became Universal-International. The phenomenally popular ABBOTT AND COSTELLO MEET FRANKENSTEIN, released by Universal-International in 1948, found Chaney as the Wolf Man, Bela Lugosi as Dracula and Glenn Strange as the Monster, as well as a fadeout gag cameo by the Invisible Man (Vincent Price) - but no Mummy. The studio seemed content to leave him under the monastery rubble which had collapsed upon him come the climax of THE MUMMY'S CURSE.

Finally, in 1955, the Mummy stirred once more at Universal-International: ABBOTT AND COSTELLO MEET THE MUMMY. The script curiously called the Mummy "Klaris," and he was played by the studio's famed horror double Eddie Parker - who had doubled Chaney as the Mummy in THE MUMMY'S TOMB. It was truly the end of the line, and the end of an era -- proving to be Abbott and Costello's final film for Universal-International.

In 1959, England's Hammer Studios, having revived the classic monsters, released *The Mummy*, starring Christopher Lee (who had just scored as Dracula and Frankenstein's Monster) in the title role. It was an exciting and stylish film, owing much of its folklore to the old Universal series. And happily, one of Universal's biggest hits of 1999 was *The Mummy*, a stylish "thrill ride" of a movie starring Brendon Fraser. The high-tech remake here and there evoked misty memories of the 1932 classic.

Lon Chaney, Jr. apparently made peace with the Mummy, whose makeup and acting opportunities had so exasperated him in the 1940s. He appeared in the Mexican opus LA CASA del TERROR (HOUSE OF TERROR) in 1959, playing a mummy (who turns into a werewolf!). And, on October 26, 1962, TV's ROUTE 66 presented its famous episode, "Lizard's Leg and Owlet's Wing," featuring

Karloff (in his Frankenstein's Monster guise), Peter Lorre (in cape and top hat) and Chaney, who appeared as the Wolfman, the Hunchback...and the Mummy.

"...I guess from the horror aspect, the character was okay," Chaney told CASTLE OF FRANKENSTEIN in 1966. He died in 1973.

Virginia Christine became one of Hollywood's busiest actresses, her scores of movies included such titles as Universal's *House of Horrors* (1946, as a "lady of the evening" killed by Rondo Hatton's "Creeper"), as well as *High Noon* (1952), *Invasion of the Body Snatchers* (1956), *Judgement at Nuremberg* (1960), *Billy the Kid vs. Dracula* (1966) and *Guess Who's Coming to Dinner* (1967). Her most familiar (and lucrative) post came as "Mrs. Olson" of the Folger's Coffee commercials - a job which made her so familiar, in fact, that her home town of Stanton, Iowa decorated its water tower to resemble a coffee pot. She was wed to character actor Fritz Feld for over 50 years, and for a time, both very popular and delightful players were the honorary mayors of Brentwood, where their home, filled with souvenirs from their careers and world travels, looked out to the ocean. Fritz Feld died in 1993. After Fritz's death, Virginia battled the results of a stroke and a heart condition. On July 24, 1996, Virginia Christine died in her sleep at her Brentwood house. Her two sons, as well as grandchildren and nieces, survived her.

And so Universal's Mummy lumbers onward. MCA Home Video has released the entire series - *The Mummy, The Mummy's Hand, The Mummy's Tomb, The Mummy's Ghost* and *The Mummy's Curse* - as well as *Abbott and Costello Meet the Mummy* - on video cassette; in fact, *...Hand, ...Tomb, ...Ghost* and *...Curse* are all packaged in a special laser disc kit.

"The odds were against it," reported VIDEO WATCHDOG when MCA/Universal released *The Mummy's Curse* on video in 1993, "but this final entry in Universal's Kharis series is the best of the lot (if you can swallow some mammoth inconsistencies)."

On late shows, on video, and in our imaginations, the Mummy roams again, still shuffling under the full moon, still seeking his reincarnated love - still charming fans of the curiously romantic, always unpretentious and delightfully fun horror series. One might suspect that Virginia Christine, in the half century that passed after her now classic mudbath in *The Mummy's Curse*, would have tired of the notoriety that always pursued her as Princess Ananka--but she insisted that wasn't so.

"After all," laughed Miss Christine, "that was one of my life experiences!"

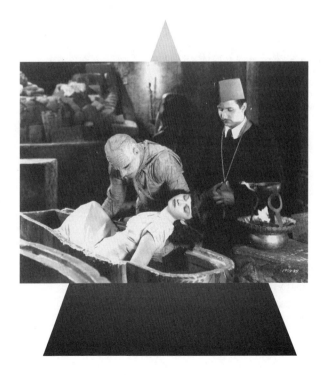

THE MUMMY'S CURSE

PRODUCER: Oliver Drake
EXECUTIVE PRODUCER: Ben Pivar
DIRECTOR: Leslie Goodwins
SCREENPLAY: Bernard L. Schubert (based on an original story, and adaptation, THE MUMMY'S RETURN, by Leon Abrams, Dwight V. Babcock, Bernard L. Schubert & T. H. Richmond)
CAMERAMAN: Virgil Miller
CAMERA OPERATOR: Bill Dodds
ASST CAMERAMAN: Frank Heisler
MUSICAL DIRECTOR: Paul Sawtell
MAKEUP: Jack P. Pierce, Joe Hadley
    Joe Bonner
HAIRDRESSER: Millissa Irwin
SPECIAL EFFECTS: John P. Fulton
    Joe McGee
ART DIRECTOR: Martin Obzina
    John B. Goodman
SET DECORATORS: Russell A. Gausman
    Victor A. Gangelin
FILM EDITOR: Fred R. Feitshans, Jr.
GOWNS: Vera West
SONG: "Hey You" - music by Oliver Drake
    lyrics by Frank Orth
LADIES WARDROBE: Molly Cook
MENS WARDROBE: Mal Caplan
ASSISTANT DIRECTORS: Mack Wright
    Joseph E. Kenny
DIALOGUE DIRECTOR: Louis Herman
CONSTRUCTION FOREMAN: Lloyd Merril
SCRIPT CLERK: Lee Frederic
SOUND DIRECTOR: Bernard B. Brown
RECORDER: Agee Kemp
MIXER: Bob Pritchard
GAFFER: Lloyd Hill
BEST BOY: Ray Fitzgerald
1ST GRIP: Charles Cowie
2ND GRIP: Charles Sheehan
MASTER OF PROPS: Ernest Smith, Jr.
2ND PROPMAN: Edward Case
PAINTER: Dennis Clarke
BOOM OPERATOR: Asa Artman

THE CAST

Kharis, the Mummy..........Lon Chaney, Jr.
Dr. Ilzor Zandaab............Peter Coe
Princess Ananka................Virginia Christine
Betty Walsh.......................Kay Harding
Halsey..............................Dennis Moore
Ragheb ....Martin Kosleck
Cajun Joe..........................Kurt Katch
Pat Walsh..........................Addison Richards
Dr. Cooper........................Holmes Herbert
Achilles............................Charles Stevens
Michael, the Sacristan........William Farnum
Goobie..............................Napoleon Simpson
Tante Berthe......................Ann Codee
Hill...................................Herbert Heywood
Ulysses.............................Tony Santoro
Pierre................................Eddie Abdo
Cajun Girl.........................Nina Bara
Bit Men.............................Herman Elliott
    Al Ferguson
Ad Lib Man........................Bud Buster
Bulldozer Driver.................Jack Lorenz

Extras & Background People

Julius Acardi, Ernest Zambrano, Saml Jereissoti, Michael Morelli, Michael Smith, Enrique Acosta, Sam Appel, George Derrick, Sam Calpriest, Isadore Isaacs, Joe Gonzales, Ray De Ravenne, Oscar Blank, Joseph Bushane, Leo Martin, Rudolph Mastro, Dario Piazza, Ernest Palmese, A. Rodriguez, Joe Rubino, Hector V. Sarno, Jose Saenz, Renato Siauss, John A. Lilley, Armand Tanny, Sid Troy, Don Alfredo, Eumenio Blanco, F. Balderrama, Armand Delmar, Elias Camboa, John Impolito, Manuel Lopez, John Marlin, Dick Stanley, Marcel Le Brun, Arthur Flavin, Art La Forest, Earl Montgomery, Silverheel Smith, Bert Cefali, Henry Carr, Steve Cavalieri, John Dako, Rod De Medici, Jay Gerard, Cliff Heard, Phil Shepard, Ted Elliott, Nick Borgani, Louis Martin, Alfredo Marin, Anthony Natale, Pepe Rodriguez, Paul Rochin, John Romano, Renato Siauss, Charles Soldani, Ernest Zambrano, Tessie Dunn, E. Daskoff, Mary Sardo, Chris Christy, Gertrude Banks, Sam Cantor, Otto Gervice, Gilbert Medina

Singers-bkgrnd music in Tante Berthe's Cafe) Emmet Casey, Buddy Clark, Mary Crouch, Austin Grout, Freeman High, Stewart Hall, Martha Manners, Lee Winters, Sidney Pepple, Stewart Blair

Double for Lon Chaney..............Robert Pepper
Double for Dennis Moore..............Carey Loftin
Double for Martin Kosleck......Teddy Mangean
Stand-In* for Peter Coe..................Joe Norden
Stand-Ins for Virginia Christine....Pauline Lane
　　　　　　　　　　　　　　　Patricia Conlin
　　　　　　　　　　　　　　　　Sally Wood
Stand-Ins for Kay Harding.............Vera Burnett
　　　　　　　　　　　　　　　　S. Weyburn
　　　　　　　　　　　　　　Agnes O'Laughlin
Stand-Ins for Dennis Moore..........Allen Goode
　　　　　　　　　　　　　　　George F. Ske
Stand-In for Martin Kosleck..........Phil Shepard
Trick Shot Stand-In for
　　Virginia Christine.......................Opal Ernie
Utility Stand-In......................Joseph Thornton

　　* The difference between a "double" and a "Stand-in:" a double actually substitutes for an actor in the finished picture, usually in action sequences; a stand-in takes the place of the actor while scenes are being set up for the camera, before the scene is shot, so not to tire the actors prior to filming.

"THE MUMMY'S RETURN"
retitled → (THE MUMMY'S CURSE)

Shooting Script

Following is the shooting script for *The Mummy's Curse* originally titled *The Mummy's Return*. The final version of the film is missing a significant amount of material which is included in this script. The notations were made by a collector and refer to these variants from the final cut of the film.

JULY 7, 1944

mr

"THE MUMMY'S RETURN"

As the CREDIT TITLES FADE OUT, to the UNDERSCORING of mood music like Debussy's "Clair de Lune," we

* FADE IN ──→ OMITTED IN FINAL DRAFT!

1   EXT. JUNGLE SWAMP AND FOREST - <u>DAY</u> - CLOSE SHOT (STOCK) - ON SWAMP

It is dark, forbidding and impenetrable. Over it is SUPERIMPOSED THE TITLE:

> "Deep in the Bayou country
> is a swampland of entangling
> vines and jungle growth..."

2 thru 5   STOCK SHOTS (TO INTERCUT)

of crocodiles slipping into the water - coveys of birds flushed from marsh land, or any other animal life indigenous to the Bayou country

                                              DISSOLVE

6   EXT. JUNGLE SWAMP AND FOREST - <u>DAY</u> - CLOSE SHOT (STOCK) - ON AN OLD GNARLED LIVEOAK OR KINDRED TREE

struggling to keep alive against entangling vines wrapped about its trunk. From a branch, Spanish moss hangs - long and thick - like a beaded oriental curtain shutting out the light. With the MUSICAL UNDERSCORING CONTINUING, OVER THE SCENE IS SUPERIMPOSED THE TITLE:

> "For countless generations it has
> remained a dwelling place of dreaded
> fears and superstition..."

                                              DISSOLVE

7   EXT. LOW SWAMPLAND - <u>DAY</u> - MED. CLOSE SHOT (STOCK) - ON SWAMPLAND

surrounded by shrubbery and glutted with wild reeds and stumps of rotted trees. With the MUSICAL UNDERSCORING CONTINUING, OVER SCENE IS SUPERIMPOSED THE TITLE:

> "...stubbornly resisting man's
> effort toward enlightenment and
> progress..."

                                              DISSOLVE

mr   2

8   CLOSE SHOT - SHRUBBERY NEAR WATER'S EDGE

dark and forbidding like the preceding scenes. Suddenly from o.s., we HEAR a cacaphoney of noises, - man-made noises of motors chugging, steam engines in operation, and the shouts and cries of men at work. INTO THE CAMERA comes crashing a bulldozer, which ruthlessly tears tangled brush apart, and floods the SCENE with sunlight, as we

DISSOLVE TO

9 thru 13   CLOSE SHOTS - A SERIES OF QUICK SCENES

a. GANG OF LABORERS, digging a water shed to catch the water drained off the swamp. Suddenly, another worker edges INTO SCENE, whispers to one. They start whispering among themselves and stop work.

b. STATIONARY ENGINE PUMP, pumping water over spillway. As the CAMERA HOLDS ON IT, the water diminishes, finally comes to an abrupt stop.

c. HEAVY STEAM ROLLER, pounding down a road - evidently being cut through the swampland. A native ENTERS SCENE, whispers to operator of the steam roller. The operator stops the roller, takes his coat and lunch pail, hops out, leaving the machine right in the middle of the road.

d. TRUCKS, being loaded with gravel and earth from a derrick.

e. DERRICK SHOVEL, loading the earth. It remains stationary in mid air.

*——↑—— END OF OMITION!

DISSOLVE TO

14   EXT. CONSTRUCTION CAMP - DAY - CLOSE SHOT - ON WOODEN SHINGLE-SIGN

bearing the lettering:

OFFICE
SOUTHERN ENGINEERING COMPANY
P. Walsh, Supt.

OVER THE INSERT we HEAR WALSH'S vehement and forceful VOICE.

CONTINUED

mr ✱ — From page 14 the scene returns to this scene! 3

14   CONTINUED

        WALSH'S VOICE O.S.
    It's up to you to get these men
    back to work!

CAMERA PANS DOWN and TRUCKS BACK to show the shingle hung
outside the entrance to the company shack. Near the porch
of this rough-hewn cabin, PAT WALSH, Superintendant, a big,
burly, construction engineer of middle age; is talking to
a group of his foremen. Among those in the group are HILL,
and elderly workman; ACHILLES, a Cajun, GOOBIE, an old
Negro workman, and ABBAS, and Egyptian, with other natives
around them.

        WALSH
    Can't these natives get it through
    their thick heads the government
    is draining that swamp for them?
      (with added emphasis)
    .. and for the sanitation and health
    of their families and children?

15   CLOSE SHOT - ON HILL

        HILL
    We're the ones who must understand,
    Mr. Walsh. The workmen are convinced
    these swamps have a curse on 'em.

16   CLOSE SHOT - ON WALSH

with others suggested around him.

        WALSH
    Don't give me any of that childish
    business, Hill...

CAMERA PANS from Walsh to Abbas who leans over to Achilles
and whispers provocatively:

        ABBAS
    Ask him - where Antoine he is?

Achilles nods, and as he turns to Walsh o.s., CAMERA TRUCKS
BACK to a WIDER ANGLE, TAKING IN the whole group, and
centering on Walsh, Achilles and Goobie.

                CONTINUED

16   CONTINUED

>   ACHILLES
> You t'ink it childish business...
> but evver'body know de place
> she'sa haunted....
>   (shrugs his shoulder)
> Antoine... he disappear last night...

>   WALSH
>   (quickly)
> Maybe he's gone over to Tante Berthe's
> Cafe and got drunk....

>   ACHILLES
> No... he no go to Tante Berthe...
> he stay on de job...Evver'body know
> who work dis swamp he ketch hard luck
> on his fam'ly an' chil'ens Chil'ens
>   (crosses himself at
>   the thought)

The workmen ad lib agreement. Goobie steps forward.

>   GOOBIE
> Achilles, he's right. On de night
> when de moon she's high in de heaven,
> de Mummy walk 'round dere...

>   ACHILLES
> Too many people... dey go in de swamp
> and nevver com out...

There is AD LIB agreement from a few of the Cajuns. We notice Abbas pulling Goobie and Achilles closer to him and whisper something to them, as though egging them on.

>   WALSH
>   (angrily)
> That's a lot of nonsense - and you
> all know it!

>   HILL
>   (conciliatingly)
> When you consider, Mr. Walsh, that the
> swamp has been the same for hundreds
> of years...

>   WALSH
>   (more impatiently)
> Then it's a good thing we've started
> doing something to remedy matters!

At this point we HEAR a car approaching. All eyes turn toward the o.s. car approaching on the gravel road that leads up to the engineering cabin.

                              CONTINUED

16   CONTINUED - 2

                    WALSH
          I don't care how you do it...

17   MED. FULL GROUP SHOT - CENTERING ON WALSH

                    WALSH
          But get those men back on the
          job, right away...
                    (with a gesture
                     of disgust)
          That's all!

The rest is lost as the car drives INTO SCENE between the CAMERA and Walsh and group. The group breaks up - workmen separating. As they leave - some with Hill; others with Abbas - Achilles heads away alone at angle toward Tante Berthe's.

18   MED. SHOW - REVERSE ANGLE

taking in the car on the road, and steps to the porch, as the workmen break up and start to EXIT FROM SCENE. Out of the car, come HALSEY, a very personable young man in his early thirties, and DR. ISMAIL FAROUK, a very distinguished-looking Egyptian of indeterminate age. CAMERA PANS WITH THE TWO MEN as Halsey, leading the way, calls:

                    HALSEY
          Mr. Walsh?....

Walsh turns, for only a moment.

                    WALSH
          Yes, what is it?

19   MED. SHOT - SHOOTING TOWARD ENTRANCE DOOR OF CABIN

as Halsey hurries up steps of porch toward Walsh, followed by Ismail.

                    HALSEY
          My name is Halsey... Dr. James Halsey
          from the Scripps Museam...
                    (indicating the scholarly
                     Egyptian beside him)
          ... and this is my colleague and
          associate, Dr. Ismail Farouk..... [Vandar]

CAMERA TRUCKS UP TO CLOSE SHOT OF THE GROUP

                                        CONTINUED

19   CONTINUED

>   WALSH
>   (continues walking
>   toward entrance to
>   his office)
> Well...what can I do for you?

CAMERA MOVES WITH THEM as Halsey, on the walk, digs down into his pocket and takes out a letter...

>   HALSEY
> I have a letter that may explain
> a great deal...

He hands the letter to Walsh, who takes it, and without even reading, opens the door and walks into his office. With an amused look between Halsey and Ismail, Halsey follows him in, as does Ismail.

20   INT. WALSH'S OFFICE - **DAY** - MED. SHOT - SHOOTING TOWARD DOOR

On his entrance, Walsh opens the letter and glances at it, while Halsey stands on one side of him and Ismail on the other. Halsey notices someone o.s. with great interest and CAMERA PANS TO THE OBJECT of his attention. Seated at a desk is BETTY, young, attractive and very intelligent-looking. She looks up from her work, not oblivious to the attractiveness of the strange caller... Consequently she smiles back (as any good secretary would do). THE CAMERA PANS BACK TO HALSEY and THE GROUP at the door.

>   WALSH
>   (with a gesture of
>   dismissal - handing
>   the letter back to Halsey)
> I don't get this at all...

Halsey, taken a little by surprise at the man's unexpected show of complete indifference, laughs... which doesn't make Walsh any friendlier.

>   WALSH (cont'd.)
> Besides... I happen to be rather
> busy...

>   HALSEY
> I merely wanted to present our
> credentials.. and ask your
> cooperation...

>   WALSH
> What for?

CONTINUED

20 CONTINUED

> HALSEY
> You're head of the Engineering
> Project here, and we've been sent
> to recover the Mummies of Kharis
> and the Princess Ananka, believed
> to be buried in these swamps....

This, apparently, is too much for Walsh, CAMERA MOVES IN
TO A TWO SHOT OF WALSH AND HALSEY, LOSING THE OTHERS.

> WALSH
> (growing madder
> by the second)
> Look, Mister, I'm having trouble
> enough with these natives and
> their silly superstition...
> (with emphasis)
> And what's more...
> (expressively)
> I won't be annoyed with a lot of
> college professors getting in my
> way!...
> (almost with
> venomous contempt)
> ...digging for Mummies!..

> HALSEY
> (more amused than
> irritated by the
> irate Walsh)
> If I promise not to get in your
> way, Mr. Walsh...

CAMERA TRUCKS BACK TO WIDER ANGLE, TAKING IN ISMAIL AND
BETTY.

> WALSH
> I'd advise you not to...

> ISMAIL
> (turns pointedly
> to Halsey)
> Dr. Halsey, has not permission been
> secured to excavate and explore these
> swamps, by the Scripps Museam?

> WALSH
> Museam or no Museam... No one's
> going to delay me!..

> HALSEY
> (cutting in just as firmly)
> You won't be delayed in the slightest.....
> In fact, Mr. Walsh, we probably won't
> start until after _your_ work is done...

CONTINUED

20   CONTINUED - 2

                    ISMAIL
          And the swamp sections are drained...

21   CLOSE TWO SHOT - BETTY AND WALSH

                    BETTY
                (looking up
                 to Walsh)
          In that case, Dr. Halsey's
          expedition won't be in our
          way at all...

                    WALSH
                (looking from Halsey o.s.
                 to Betty)
          You stay out of this...

                    BETTY
                (to Walsh)
          Just becuase you're upset is no
          reason to be unfriendly to them...

22   MED. GROUP SHOT

      showing Halsey's reaction as he turns from Walsh and
      Betty and Ismail...

                    WALSH
                (cutting in)
          I've had enough argument for
          one day...
                (then all business;
                 starts walking away,
                 to Betty)
          Don't forget to follow up on
          that requisition for cable and
          another derrick...
                (turns to Halsey
                 and Ismail)
          Good day, Gentlemen...
                (grabs hat)
          I'll be back in a second, Betty...

      Walsh EXITS, Halsey watches the excitable man disappear
      from SCENE, then turns back to Betty.

23   CLOSE TWO SHOT - HALSEY AND BETTY

                    HALSEY
          Thanks for helping us out... but you
          shouldn't talk back to your Boss like
          that... You're liable to get fired....

                                                  CONTINUED

23 CONTINUED

> BETTY
> (lightly)
> You mustn't mind Uncle Pat..

> HALSEY
> (reacting)
> Your Uncle?

> BETTY
> (nods)
> He isn't nearly as unpleasant as he appears to be... It's only that we've been having so much trouble with native superstition...

> HALSEY
> (with a smile)
> That's nothing new to us, is it, Ismail?...

CAMERA TRUCKS BACK TO TAKE IN ISMAIL

> ISMAIL
> (curtly turns to her)
> In Archaeology, Miss Walsh.. one always experiences the same trouble...

> BETTY
> (after a slight pause; to Halsey)
> Archaeology is a very interesting subject..I took a year of it at college...

> HALSEY
> (immediately interested; draws closer to her)
> Say, we have something in common, haven't we?

From o.s. thay HEAR Walsh's voice:

> WALSH VOICE O.S.
> What makes you so sure, Dr. Halsey...

They turn and look.

24 CLOSE SHOT - ON WALSH

He has just returned and is still wearing his hat.

> WALSH
> ....that the Mummy Prince and Princess are buried in the swamps here?

CONTINUED

mr   10

24   CONTINUED

        CAMERA PANS WITH HIM as he approaches the group.

                        HALSEY
                Because, many years ago, the Mummy
                had run off with a girl from this
                locality... Pursued by the natives
                and Sheriff's posse, he made for the
                swamps at the foot of the Mahoozis
                River....

                                                DISSOLVE OUT

        DISSOLVE IN * (STOCK FOOTAGE NOT INCLUDED IN "SHORT" NARA-
                       TIVE OF THE MUMMY'S PAST EXISTANCE)

25   SCENE 75, (STOCK) - "THE MUMMY'S GHOST" - VIEW OF INCLINE
        AND SHACK.

        Men running up incline - Kharis descending ladder with Amina

26   SCENE 76, (STOCK) - CLOSE VIEW TRAVELING SHOT ON INCLINE

        Man running up - EXITS.

27   SCENE 77, (STOCK) - LOWER PART OF STRUCTURE

        Kharis at foot of ladder with Amina.

28   SCENE 78, (STOCK) - CLOSEUP - EXT. OPEN DOOR

        Walgreen comes on - EXITS inside. Sheriff and deputies
        follow - EXIT inside.

29   SCENE 90, (STOCK) - CLOSE SHOT - ALONG BRUSHY SLOPE

        Kharis carrying Amina toward b.g.

30   SCENE 94, (STOCK) - CLOSE SHOT - EDGE OF MARSH

        Kharis carrying Amina toward ground which is softening.

31   SCENE 95, (STOCK) - LARGE CLOSEUP - KHARIS' LEG

        as it moves along, bringing more of his body INTO SCENE.
        Withered arm swinging down. ALL EXIT.

32   SCENE 96, (STOCK) - CLOSE SHOT - IN MARSH

        Peanuts runs across thru mire - barking.

33   SCENE 98, (STOCK) - CLOSE VIEW - OF RIVER BOTTOM

        Kharis carrying Amina - moves across.

  34   SCENE 99, (STOCK) - LARGE CLOSEUP - IN RIVER BOTTOM

        Kharis comes partly into scene, carrying body of old woman
        - feet and legs withered and shrunken - starts to EXIT.

  35   SCENE 102, (STOCK) - CLOSE SHOT - IN RIVER BOTTOM

        Kharis carrying Amina thru slender saplings toward b.g.

  36   SCENE 106 - (STOCK) - CLOSE SHOT - RIVER BANK

        Kharis carrying Amina toward b.g.

  37   SCENE 109, (STOCK) - CLOSE SHOT - RIVER BOTTOM

        Kharis carrying Amina toward b.g.

  38   SCENE 110, (STOCK) - MED. SHOT - RIVER BANK

        Kharis carries Amina down into water.

  39   SCENE 117, (STOCK) - LARGE CLOSEUP REAR VIEW OF KHARIS

        Carrying Amina thru water.

  40   SCENE 119, (STOCK) - CLOSE SHOT - RIVER

        Kharis and Amina almost submerged.

  41   SCENE 120, (STOCK) - LARGE CLOSEUP - AMINA

        Face shrivelled and old.

  42   SCENE 122, (STOCK) - CLOSE VIEW - SIDE OF RIVER

        Kharis and Amina almost completely under water.

  43   SCENE 123, (STOCK) - LARGE CLOSEUP - AMINA'S FACE

        Shrivelled and old - EXITS under water.

  44   SCENE 126, (STOCK) - CLOSE SHOT - RIVER

        No sign of life.

                                              DISSOLVE BACK TO

45 INT. WALSH'S OFFICE - <u>DAY</u> - GROUP SHOT - CENTERING ON
    HALSEY

with Betty listening eagerly, and Ismail nodding assent,
Walsh has a look of disgust on his face.

                HALSEY
              (to Walsh)
And that, my friend, is a matter of
record....
              (with a look to
              Betty)
The newspaper files of the Bayou Times
carried long descriptive accounts
of the event....

                WALSH
              (to Halsey)
Do you expect me to believe anything
as fantastic as that?

                ISMAIL
              (answering with
              a smile)
In the Dicta of the Fathers it is
written..."Truth will flourish in
fantasy, only to wither and die,
in what you occidentals are pleased
to call...'reality'"....

                HALSEY
Speaking of reality... I think it's
time we got organized, Ismail....

He turns as if to go, when suddenly from the entrance they
HEAR someone approaching, hurriedly. The door opens and
GOOBIE comes RUNNING INTO SCENE.

                GOOBIE
              (frightened)
Mr. Walsh!.. Mr. Walsh! Sumpin'
turrible happen....

                WALSH
              (impatiently)
What is it now, Goobie?

                GOOBIE
Antoine...they foun' him... daid...

The others are alarmed at this news. Walsh approaches
the old colored workman.

                WALSH
              (angrily)
What?

                              CONTINUED

45   CONTINUED

> GOOBIE
> (excitedly)
> At de edge of de pit -- on de odder side of de swamp.
>
> WALSH
> Another one of those unnecessary accidents, I suppose.
>
> GOOBIE
> (somewhat apprehensively)
> No, suh... He wuz killed...

All react to this and Ismail listens intently as Goobie continues.

> GOOBIE
> De workmen all mighty scared, suh -- dey gonna quit!
>
> WALSH
> (grimly) CAGEY
> Well get hold of Big Joe -- he's probably at Tante Berthe's cafe.
>
> GOOBIE
> Yes, suh.
>
> WALSH
> (to Halsey)
> He knows how to handle these people - and they listen to him.
> (to Goobie)
> Find Joe and bring him to the big pit <u>right away</u>.
>
> GOOBIE
> Yes, suh.

Goobie turns and hurries OUT OF SCENE.* (To Page 17!)

DISSOLVE

*— OPENING OF FILM!

46   * EXT. TANTE BERTHE'S CAFE - <u>NIGHT</u> - CLOSE SHOT - ON BIG JOE

He is a mammoth man with the bright, sparkling eyes of a Latin. He is a former Portugese pearl fisherman, now employed as gang foreman for Walsh.

CONTINUED

— ↓ — Beginning of film starts here! Some dialogue is changed around or completely omitted.

46   CONTINUED

As we COME IN on Joe, he is up at the bar with drink in hand, laughing uproariously, while from o.s. we HEAR the SOUND OF MEN talking in curious dialects, and MUSIC and SINGING. As we TRUCK BACK from Big Joe at the bar to the interior of TANTE BERTHE'S CAJUN CAFE, we SEE a quaint and colorful meeting place, presumably on the edge of the swampland in the Bayou country. All about are clustered the native workmen and others, Achilles among them. They stand around either smoking their pipes, talking, playing cards, or joining in the singing, as accompaniment to TANTE BERTHE herself, an ample-bosomed, generous and kindly woman in her thirties (though she looks older), indegenous to the soil about her. She is singing one of the quaint Cajun folk songs, "A Fais-dodo", to the accompaniment of an accordian. The NUMBER IS COMPLETED to a burst of spontaneous applause and further animated talking and drinking. As Tante Berthe finishes, she moves toward Big Joe, and he roars out over the raucous sound of other talk.

                    BIG JOE
          Tante Berthe, you sing plentee
          fin'....Maybe some day you get
          tired being wife to little guy...

He indicates and CAMERA PANS WITH HIM to take in a little insignificant Cajun, dwarfed in comparison to Big Joe's size.

                    BIG JOE
                    (cont'd)
          Ulysses, and his nineteen
          chillun....

ULYSSES smiles, proud of this compliment to his virility... and immediately starts naming them.

                    ULYSSES
          Odile, Odellia, Odalia, Olive,
          Oliver, Olivia, Ophelia, Odelia....

CAMERA PANS BACK TO A MED. SHOT - CENTERING ON BIG JOE

                    BIG JOE
          Enuff....That's enuff...
                    (turns back to
                    Tante Berthe)
          Then you marry me, eh, Tante Berthe?

                                        CONTINUED

46 CONTINUED - 2

> TANTE BERTHE
> It ain't much fun be' married
> twice as old as yourself to a
> man, no?

Those standing around laugh at this joke.

> BIG JOE
> (kidding her)
> Yeah, but some day purty soon
> I be rich man...

> TANTE BERTHE
> (coquettishly)
> You maka so much money, gang
> foreman in swamp clearin'?

> BIG JOE
> When the job she'sa feenished in
> the swamp clearing, I tak' my
> money, and get me good pearl fishin'
> groun's in Bayou Barataria....

Achilles speaks up.

> ACHILLES
> The work in de swamp she'sa
> feenish now...

Instantly, the attention of the others is drawn to these two people.

> BIG JOE
> (turns to him)
> What for you say dat?

> ACHILLES
> 'Cause nobody, she'sa so foolish
> to work dere...and you know why...

> BIG JOE
> (trying to ridicule
> him)
> No. Achilles... you tell me why....

> ACHILLES
> On the night when the moon she'sa
> high in heaven... the Mummy and
> his Princess they walk....
> (crosses himself)

> BIG JOE
> (laughing aloud)
> Crazee...fooleesh....

CONTINUED

46   CONTINUED - 3

PIERRE, another Cajun workman, speaks out.

> PIERRE
> Antoine...Where he is? Eh?....
> Maybe Mummy got him?....

Other Cajuns react quickly.

> ACHILLES
> The Loup-garou they no wan' no
> more diggin' in de swamp... I go
> back pick moss...but no worka in the
> swamp....nevaire...

Others begin to AD LIB freely, discussing it.... With the exception of Big Joe, all agree that no good would come of working in the swamps.

> AD LIBS
> He needer....
> I no go to de place...
> Achilles, he'sa right...
> The place...she'sa haunt....

47   CLOSE SHOT - BIG JOE (OTHERS SUGGESTED IN B.G.)

> BIG JOE
> (silencing them)
> Wait...Stop...You listen to me...
> I know better from all of you....
> I be pearl fishin8 this place more
> dan thirty year... Long ago there
> was a Mummy like you say....

The others react as he continues.

> BIG JOE
> And he take a girl in the swamp...

Others look from one to the other, wondering whether to be frightened or whether this is just another one of Big Joe's famous jokes.

> BIG JOE
> That'sa true... I no foolin'....
> but that has been twenty-five year
> past....

* — End of film opening

48   MED. ANGLE SHOT - CENTERING ON BIG JOE

leaning over the bar, with Tante Berthe facing him across the bar. Others are suggested in the b.g.

CONTINUED

48   CONTINUED

                    BIG JOE
          The Mummy's spirit he'sa never
          bodder me an I pass over his head
          hund'ed maybe t'ousan' times....
          And maybe even I tickla' his ribs
          when I dig for the oyster... Then
          he have a good laugh.

     He laughs at his own joke. The others don't seem to
     appreciate his comedy.

                    BIG JOE
          Don' worry my fr'ens....

49   CLOSE SHOT - ON BIG JOE

                    BIG JOE
          So you have not to be 'fraid
          from heem....

*   Just at this point, there is great excitement as the o.s.
     door opens. We HEAR GOOBIE'S VOICE:
     (Continued from page 13.-
                    GOOBIE'S VOICE O.S.
               Master (highly excited)
          ~~Big~~ Joe!...Big Joe!... Massa Walsh
          lookin' fer yuh....

50   WIDER ANGLE - MED. SHOT - TAKING IN THE EXCITED GOOBIE
         NEAR DOOR AND BIG JOE AT BAR

                    GOOBIE
          ...and he raisin' holy ned...

                    BIG JOE
          What he wanta me for?

51   CLOSE SHOT - GOOBIE.

                    GOOBIE
               (with a fanatical look;
               his eyes bulging with
               excitement)
          Fin' a lizard on de grave...
          'Taint no charm yo' life would save...

52   MED. SHOT - ON GROUP

     Everybody looks at Goobie

                    BIG JOE
          Hey, what you talkin' about
          Goobie?

                                                  CONTINUED

52 CONTINUED

>   GOOBIE
>   Dey's foun' Antoine... wid a knife
>   in his back...

The others are held in silent fear.

>   GOOBIE
>   (continuing)
>   An' dat ain't all. Massa Walsh
>   want me to fetch you to de
>   big pit.

Big Joe and Goobie EXIT, CAMERA PANNING with them.

>   DISSOLVE

53 EXT. EXCAVATION PIT IN SWAMPS - <u>NIGHT</u> - MED. FULL SHOT - ON GROUP OF WORKMEN

standing in silent awe near a bulldozer. CAMERA PANS from the bulldozer on down to where Halsey, Walsh, Betty, Hill, Achilles, Goobie, Ismail, Abbas and Big Joe are gathered about the body of Antoine, sprawled on the ground near bottom of pit, the end of a knife protruding from his back. The onlookers carry lanterns and flashlights. As Halsey, Walsh, Hill, Big Joe and Goobie move forward to examine the body, Hill speaks.

>   HILL
>   I don't know how this could've
>   happened during the day -- with
>   the men working all around here.

54 MED. CLOSE SHOT - ON GROUP AROUND ANTOINE - X-ING OUT THE BODY

>   WALSH
>   (harshly)
>   Antoine has been missing all day -
>   so he must've been murdered last
>   night - and the body left here.

>   GOOBIE
>   (fanatically)
>   De debbil's on de loose! -- mebbee
>   so we all be killed!

As the assembled workmen o.s. AD LIB apprehensive comments, Big Joe whirls on Goobie.

                                        CONTINUED

54 CONTINUED

> BIG JOE
> Keepa you face shut, Goobie!

Goobie subsides in awe. Then as all glance back toward Antoine's body o.s., Halsey, who has been looking about, suddenly whirls and stares wide-eyed toward the o.s. pit. CAMERA PANS SLOWLY OVER and DOWN to a distinct indentation in the clay pit of a man's body, with arms and legs extended. Halsey steps INTO SCENE past Camera, and as his flashlight and the beams of other lights hit the indentation, he kneels down to examine it.

(DIALOGUE MISSING!)

55 MED. SHOT - REVERSE ANGLE - SHOOTING OVER THE HEADS AND SHOULDERS OF WALSH, BIG JOE, BETTY, HILL, GOOBIE AND A COUPLE OF OTHER WORKMEN - TO HALSEY

kneeling over the imprint of the huge body in the clay pit. Ismail and Betty move forward to crowd about him.

> WALSH
> (puzzled)
> Looks like the imprint of a man's body, Halsey.

56 CLOSE SHOT - ON HALSEY, WALSH, ISMAIL AND BETTY - ANGLE SHOOTING PAST THEIR TENSE FACES - TO THE INDENTATION IN THE PIT

> HALSEY
> (excitedly)
> Not a man's body, Mr. Walsh. Unless I'm wrong, a mummy was buried here -- until the bulldozer uncovered it.

Halsey emphasizes his words by reaching down and picking up some molded wrapping of mummy cloth. He holds it up for Ismail to see.

> HALSEY
> What do you make of this, Ismail?

Ismail turns his flashlight on the mummy wrapping in Halsey's hand.

> ISMAIL
> (thoughtfully)
> It might be part of the wrapping from a mummy - but it would take a full microscopic test to make certain.

CONTINUED

56   CONTINUED

As all react to this, excited AD LIB comments go up from o.s.

57   MED. CLOSE SHOT - ON GOOBIE - INCLUDING BIG JOE, ACHILLES, HILL, ISMAIL AND OTHER WORKMEN

> GOOBIE
> De debbil8s on de loose - an' dancin' wid de mummy!

> ACHILLES
> (fearfully)
> You see what I tol' you, Beeg Joe - the Loup-garou he'sa plenty mad. Only crazee people a-dig in the swamp.

> WORKMEN
> (ad lib)
> He'sa right.
> De swamp she'sa haunt by de mummy.

> BIG JOE
> How many times I tolda you the mummy he'sa no scare nobody?

All look from Big Joe toward Halsey and others o.s.

58   MED. SHOT - ON HALSEY, BETTY, WALSH AND ISMAIL

as they get to their feet near indentation of the mummy, with Halsey still holding on to the mummy wrapping.

> HALSEY
> If this cloth wrapping did come from the mummy, then whoever found it must've murdered Antoine.

> WALSH
> (scoffing)
> Stuff and nonsense! The whole story's fantastic!

> HALSEY
> Perhaps it's not as fantastic as it seems, Mr. Walsh.

Walsh snorts, then turns and EXITS from scene. We hear him calling out:

CONTINUED

58   CONTINUED

>   WALSH'S VOICE O.S.
>   (calling out)
>   Big Joe! - have some of the men take
>   Antoine's body back to town and
>   notify the authorities!

During this dialogue, CAMERA DOLLIES IN to a CLOSEUP on the mummy wrapping in Halsey's hand:

                                                DISSOLVE

→ OPENING SCENE BEGINS ON PAGE 24

59   INT. HALSEY'S LABORATORY TENT - <u>DAY</u> - CLOSEUP - ON MUMMY WRAPPING - ON A WORK TABLE

CAMERA DOLLIES SLOWLY BACK to disclose Halsey seated at table, examining the mummy wrapping under a microscope. He is intent on his study, when suddenly we hear BETTY'S O.S. VOICE behind him,

>   BETTY'S VOICE O.S.
>   May I come in?

Dr. Halsey is so intent he doesn't hear it at first.

>   BETTY'S VOICE O.S.
>   (calling again - louder)
>   Hello, there!....May I come in?

>   HALSEY
>   (without looking up)
>   Yes..Come in...come in...

Betty ENTERS THE SCENE and approaches. When Halsey, looking up from the microscope discovers who it is, he quickly gets to his feet, CAMERA TRUCKS IN CLOSER.

>   HALSEY
>   Oh...I'm sorry...

>   BETTY
>   I hope I'm not disturbing you...
>   I....

                                                CONTINUED

59   CONTINUED

Halsey beckons her over to the microscope, CAMERA TRUCKS IN TO A CLOSE TWO SHOT OF HALSEY AND BETTY

> HALSEY
> You're interested in archaeology...
> Take a look at that...

> BETTY
> (looking into
> microscope)
> What an interesting pattern!
> Looks like gorgeous lace...

> HALSEY
> The Egyptians knew their cotton...
> and how to weave it...thousands of
> years ago....

> BETTY
> (looking up)
> Thousands of years....

> HALSEY
> That's mummy cloth...found in
> the excavation...

CAMERA PANS WITH HIM as he walks her to laboratory table, over to one side. There on the table before them is a piece of earthen clay, broken off into part of a mold.

> HALSEY
> Take a good look at this
> impression...What part of the
> Mummy's body would you say it is?

> BETTY
> I don't know...but it looks as
> if it might be the skull...

> HALSEY
> Right...the first time....

60   CLOSE SHOT - SHOOTING OVER HALSEY'S SHOULDER - ON BETTY

She is definitely interested in this young archaeologist...

> BETTY
> (with admiration)
> Wonderful, how quickly you've
> been able to find a clew....

61   CLOSE SHOT - ON HALSEY - BETTY SILHOUETTED IN B.G.

>   HALSEY
>   (disappointedly)
>   We've certainly done all right...
>   We find a clew... and lose the
>   Mummy...

62   CLOSE TWO SHOT - ON HALSEY AND BETTY

>   BETTY
>   Isn't it the strangest thing
>   how it could have disappeared?
>
>   HALSEY
>   Well, if it's old Kharis, he'll
>   soon make his presence felt...
>
>   BETTY
>   Kharis?
>
>   HALSEY
>   That's the name of the Mummy...
>   (obviously changing
>   the subject)
>   By the way, I never thanked you
>   for getting your Uncle Pat to
>   drain this section first...
>
>   BETTY
>   (modestly)
>   Aren't you exaggerating my
>   influence?
>
>   HALSEY
>   (looking at her
>   intently)
>   You're gorgeously... beautifully...
>
>   BETTY
>   (a little surprised)
>   I beg your pardon...
>
>   HALSEY
>   Non-committal.....

They both laugh... She walks around, looking over the
Laboratory, Halsey with her. CAMERA TRUCKS WITH THEM.

>   BETTY
>   You're very well equipped here..
>   aren't you?..... And everything
>   is so neatly arranged...

                                                    CONTINUED

62   CONTINUED

> HALSEY
> Now you're giving _me_ too much credit...
> (waxing suddenly
> enthusiastic)
> My assistant is a perfect pearl of
> reliability... and efficiency...
> (calls out)
> Ismail!!...

They turn to face the door. There is no answer.

> HALSEY
> (calling again)
> Ismail!!!...

Receiving no answer, he walks toward door and calls across toward Ismail's tent o.s.

> HALSEY
> Ismail!!!
> (turns back to Betty)
> That's what I get for bragging
> too much...

He walks back to Betty.

> BETTY
> You can't always expect him to be
> at your beck and call...

> HALSEY
> That's strange... I suppose I am
> spoiled... but nothing like this
> ever happened before...
> (turns to call
> again)
> Ismail!!!...

CONTINUATION FROM PAGE 21!   DISSOLVE

63   EXT. MISTY SWAMP - <u>NIGHT</u> - CLOSE MOVING SHOT

Ismail is standing in a dugout boat, poling his way carefully between treacherous stumps that stand silent as ghouls in the night. He makes his way to the shore of the swampland, shielded and hidden by overgrown bushes and peers into the darkened night mysteriously, as if expecting someone. He hops out of the dugout and carefull hides it in the shrubbery and tall grass. As he does so, unbeknownst to himself, the shrubbery on <u>either side of him</u> suddenly begins to quake and agitate with movement. <u>HEARING</u> it, Ismail quickly gets to his feet and twirls around, to face the moving shrubbery on one side... As he does so, the CAMERA QUICKLY SWINGS OVER to the other side of him where the shrubbery is also in motion.

64   MED. SHOT (STOCK) - <u>NIGHT</u> - ON A CROCODILE

   making its way from the shore as if it had just crept out from the shrubbery, to slip into the water, with a splash.

65   CLOSE SHOT - FROM ANOTHER ANGLE - ON ISMAIL

   Attracted to the splashing SOUND, he turns to see the crocodile swimming off in the water. Suddenly, out of the bushes from the other side of him, looms the figure of Abbas, axe in hand, looking around menacingly.

>   ABBAS
>   (calling in excited
>   whispers)
>   Master!... Master!...

   Ismail turns with a start, but regains his composure quickly as he faces Abbas.

>   ISMAIL
>   'Tis you, Abbas...
>
>   ABBAS
>   Yes, Master...
>
>   ISMAIL
>   The hours of night are few...
>   Lead the way, quickly...

   As Abbas starts hacking their way through the brambles, Ismail follows after him.

66   MED. CLOSE SHOT - ON A HIDDEN PATH

   leading up to a hill. CAMERA SHOOTS DOWN TO THE SWAMP EDGE, as Abbas, hacking his way, ENTERS SCENE, followed by Ismail, approaching CAMERA.

>   ABBAS
>   (indicating
>   path)
>   See, Master... The hidden path,
>   as though by miracle leads right
>   up the hill from the very swamp
>   edge.

   Ismail stops him.

67   CLOSE SHOT - ISMAIL AND ABBAS

                    ISMAIL
               (looking around)
          But the Mummy cases... Where are
          they?

                    ABBAS
               (proud of
                 himself)
          Safely hidden in the Monastery...

                    ISMAIL
               (surprised)
          You couldn't have carried them
          up, alone...

                    ABBAS
          I've had help...

                    ISMAIL
               (immediately
                 concerned)
          You were warned to work secretly...

                    ABBAS
               (meaningfully
                 and with
                 confidence)
          Those who helped will not talk...

                    ISMAIL
          They were silenced, I trust,
          less noticeably than the native,
          Antoine...

                    ABBAS
               (apologetically)
          I had to act quickly, Master...

Ismail silences him with a gesture... They continue without
speaking for a moment...

                    ABBAS
               (gloatingly)
          This time, their bones will
          long be turned to powder before
          our secret is discovered...

                                        CONTINUED

67   CONTINUED

If Abbas is expecting any expression of praise from Ismail, he is doomed to disappointment. Ismail merely looks up and starts walking again up the hill.

> ISMAIL
> The hours do not linger...

As he continues on PAST CAMERA, Abbas soberly follows.

68   EXT. MONASTERY - <u>NIGHT</u> - LONG SHOT - SHOOTING UP TEMPLE STEPS

overgrown with weeds and broken stones, now bathed in moonlight. Ismail ENTERS SCENE with Abbas. As they stand there, Abbas speaks:

> ABBAS
> There it is, Master...built by Spanish Padres centuries ago...

(* Following Not Used!)

> ISMAIL
> (pointing off)
> Wait...until I summon you....

Abbas waits over to one side as Ismail walks to the first step. He then stops to look up, prayerfully.

> ISMAIL
> To the great God, Amon-Ra....
> King of all the Gods...Accept this prayer of thanks for leading us to this place...where we may fulfill our tasks for thee...
> (slight pause; then turns and calls)
> Abbas....

Abbas ENTERS SCENE and joins him. As they walk up the steps, we

End omission!

> DISSOLVE

69   INT. MONASTERY - <u>NIGHT</u> - MED. SHOT - ON CEREMONIAL ROOM

once probably a chapel in the old Monastery, it is now a dim, vaulted, forbidding room with stone floor and dark walls. (much like the interior of the temple in "The Mummy's Hand").

CONTINUED

69   CONTINUED

Over to one side is a stone table, while two Mummy cases lie flat on the floor nearby. All is in silence, when suddenly WE HEAR a heavy door creak on its hinges. THE CAMERA PANS TOWARD IT. It slowly opens. Leading the way is Abbas, with lighted torch in hand, followed by Ismail. CAMERA PANS BACK WITH THEM, as they ENTER the room.

* Short dialogue missing!

                    ISMAIL
           But where is Kharis?

                    ABBAS
           This way, Master...

He walks over towards the first mummy case on the floor, stops at the head of it, holds up the light.

70   CLOSE SHOT - SHOOTING DOWN ON THE MUMMY

as the flaming torch o.s. casts weird moving shadows that play upon the Mummy's face, in grotesque, frightening patterns. Kharis is in soiled Mummy wrappings, and presumably in a state of suspended animation...

71   CLOSE GROUP SHOT - ISMAIL AND ABBAS

with Mummy case between them.

                    ISMAIL
              (looking up from
               Mummy)
           (From Page 29!) And where's the copper box...
           and the sacred brazier?

                    ABBAS
           Here, Master...

CAMERA TRUCKS BACK TO WIDER SHOT as he crosses over to a fixture at side, holding the bowl in which the Tana leaves are brewed, — as in every Mummy picture.

                                        CONTINUED

71   CONTINUED

                              ISMAIL
                      (still standing over
                      Mummy case; to Abbas)
                 Kharis will soon be ready to return
                 to life and movement...
                      (to Mummy)
                 Yes, Kharis, you shall rise again...
                 to find your Princess Ananka...
                 That is our vow to you!
         *—— SHORT SPEECH MISSING; RETURN TO PAGE 28!
                              ABBAS
                      (indicating copper
                      chest)
                 And this, is the box...

        Ismail crosses to the box.
              (Return from Page 28!)
                              ISMAIL
                 Open it...

        Abbas opens box.

                              ISMAIL
                 There you will find leaves of
                 the ancient Tana tree.

                              ABBAS
                 Yes, Master...

                              ISMAIL
                 Bring three to me...

72   CLOSE SHOT - ON ABBAS

        selecting three leaves. CAMERA CROSSES WITH HIM TO ISMAIL

73   CLOSE TWO SHOT - ISMAIL AND ABBAS

        as Ismail puts leaves in the brazier.

                              ISMAIL
                 Three to keep his heart beating...

74   CLOSE SHOT - ON ISMAIL

        as he looks off toward the Mummy case.

                              ISMAIL
                 Once each night, during the cycle
                 of the full moon, we will dissolve
                 three Tana leaves and give the
                 fluid to Kharis.

75   CLOSE TWO SHOT - ISMAIL AND ABBAS

                    ABBAS
              (as tho repeating a
               lesson to be learned)
        Yes, Master...Once each night during
        the cycle of the full moon...

                    ISMAIL
        And nine leaves each night to
        give life and movement...

76   CLOSE SHOT - ON ABBAS

                    ABBAS
              (repeating to
               memorize)
        Yes, Master, nine leaves each night
        to give him life and movement...

77   CLOSE TWO SHOT - ISMAIL AND ABBAS

        as Ismail hands Abbas a medallion.

                    ISMAIL
        Now by this medallion of the lay
        Priests of ~~Karnak~~ ARKAN, you will swear
        to the ancient gods of Egypt that
        you will not betray your trust...

78   INSERT: CLOSE SHOT OF MEDALLION

        in the hands of Abbas.

                    ABBAS' VOICE O.S.
        I swear by the mighty power of
        Amon-Ra....whose anger can shatter
        the world...

79   CLOSE TWO SHOT - ISMAIL AND ABBAS

                    ABBAS
        ...that I will not betray my
        trust.

        By this time the juice is boiling and steam is rising
        from the brazier.

                    ISMAIL
        Now that you have sworn...the time
        has come when you must know the
        purpose of our mission.

        Ismail turns toward the brazier...

vc   31

80   CLOSE SHOT - ON BRAZIER

      from which steam is rising.

                                ISMAIL'S VOICE O.S.
                          Come and look back with me across
                          the years...that pass as vapor
                          before thine eyes...

      The steam of the brazier fills the screen.

                                               DISSOLVE TO

81   SCENE 15 - (STOCK) - MED. SHOT - INT. TEMPLE

      Vapor parts, disclosing Scene in ancient temple,
      attendants serving Princess.

                                ISMAIL'S VOICE O.S.
                          Over three thousand years ago,
                          the Princess Ananka...

                                                  DISSOLVE

      VIEW OF RUGGED MOUNTAINSIDE - (STOCK)
      Funeral procession passing along path toward foot of
      slope - attendants dancing.

                                ISMAIL'S VOICE O.S.
                          ...died. She was buried with all
                          the ceremony due her.

82   SCENE 16 - CLOSE SHOT ON PATH - (STOCK)   MUSIC

      Immense catafalque on sledge - slaves passing it.

                                ISMAIL'S VOICE O.S.
                          Ananka's father, King Amenophis, bid
                          her a last farewell.

83   SCENE 17 - CORRIDOR IN TOMB (STOCK)

      Soldiers standing with burning torches - slaves come on
      with coffin - carry it toward b.g.   MUSIC-CHANTING

                                                  DISSOLVE

      INT. UNDERGROUND TOMB (STOCK)
      Slaves and soldiers standing with blazing torches -
      slaves carry coffin toward f.g.

                                                 CONTINUED

83   CONTINUED

                    ISMAIL'S VOICE O.S.
            And thus, the Princess Ananka was
            placed in her tomb.

84   SCENE 18 - CLOSE SHOT - INT. TOMB (STOCK)

      Kharis and two soldiers standing - holding torches -
      the end of the Mummy case comes on at side - MUSIC-CHANTING

                    ISMAIL'S VOICE O.S.
            Kharis, a Prince of the Royal house,
            who loved Ananka, looked on in grief.

85   SCENE 19 - CLOSEUP - KHARIS (STOCK)

      Looking off - grieving - bows his head. MUSIC-CHANTING

                    ISMAIL'S VOICE O.S.
            His devotion was so great that he
            refused to believe that she was
            lost to him forever.

86   SCENE 20 - INT. TOMB (STOCK)

      Ceremonies going on - men go toward b.g. with torches

                                          MUSIC-CHANTING

87   SCENE 21 - MED. CLOSE SHOT - STATUE OF ISIS (STOCK)

      Kharis standing below the statue - touches the base.
      Panel slides open.

                    ISMAIL'S VOICE O.S.
            Kharis broke into the altar room
            of Isis to steal the Secret of
            Eternal Life...

88   SCENE 22 - CLOSEUP - BASE OF STATUE (STOCK)

      Chest in base - panel open - Kharis comes on - looks
      around fearfully - draws out the chest - removes the
      cover - disclosing a mass of dried leaves - picks up
      handful of them - looks up.

                                          CONTINUED

88   CONTINUED

                    ISMAIL'S VOICE O.S.
              ...from its hiding place. With that,
              he knew he could bring Ananka back to
              life. Daring the anger of the ancient
              gods, he stole the forbidden Tana leaves.

89   SCENE 23 - CLOSEUP - STATUE OF ISIS (STOCK)

      Camera moves from feet to hand - arm of statue moves
                                        MUSIC

                                        DISSOLVE TO

      CLOSEUP - MUMMY CASE (STOCK)
      The top sitting cross-wise over the lower part in
      which the body is seen. CAMERA MOVES BACK partly dis-
      closing kneeling man. *- NARRATIVE CUT FROM FILM BEGINNING HERE!

90   SCENE 24 - CLOSEUP - KHARIS (STOCK)

      Kneeling - hears something - looks around - MUSIC

91   SCENE 25 - MED. CLOSE - IN THE TOMB (STOCK)

      Kharis kneeling in f.g. - soldiers and priest ENTER in b.g.

92   SCENE 26 - CLOSEUP - KHARIS (STOCK)

      Frowning - starts to rise -

93   SCENE 27 - MED. CLOSE - IN THE TOMB (STOCK)

      Kharis rises - guards in b.g., ancient scroll unrolled
      on the floor - casket with cover crosswise - Kharis
      goes to b.g.
                                        DISSOLVE TO

      MED. PAN SHOT - IN THE TEMPLE (STOCK)
      Guards and slaves standing about - King on the throne -
      Kharis stands before him.

94   SCENE 28 - CLOSEUP - KING (STOCK)

      Seated on throne - moves hands -   MUSIC

                    ISMAIL'S VOICE O.S.
              For the sin he hath committed...

95   SCENE 29 - CLOSEUP - KHARIS (STOCK)

Horrified - he hears: *(Return Narrative) MUSIC

      ISMAIL'S VOICE O.S.
  Kharis was condemned to be
  buried alive....

           DISSOLVE TO

LARGE CLOSEUP - KHARIS' HEAD (STOCK)
Bandages being wrapped around it - eyes staring.

      ISMAIL'S VOICE O.S.
  But first they cut out his tongue
  so the ears of the Gods would not
  be assailed by his unholy curses.

           DISSOLVE TO

CLOSE SHOT - IN THE TOMB (STOCK)
Slaves pick up bandaged body - Priest and soldiers in b.g.
Slaves place body in casket in f.g. CAMERA MOVES BACK.
Slaves start to put cover on casket -   MUSIC-CHANTING

           DISSOLVE TO

MED. SHOT - ON HILLSIDE (STOCK)
Priest, soldiers and slaves, etc., walking by the light
of blazing torches - casket is carried to f.g. by slaves.

      ISMAIL'S VOICE O.S.
  But sinful Kharis...

96   SCENE 30 - CLOSE VIEW ON THE PATH (STOCK)

Slaves carrying heavy casket - they set it down -

          MUSIC-CHANTING

      ISMAIL'S VOICE O.S.
  ...was buried alone in a remote spot.

97   SCENE 31 - MED. CLOSE - ON HILLSIDE (STOCK)

Priest and soldiers watching as slaves put casket in
tomb -   MUSIC-CHANTING

98   SCENE 32 - CLOSE SHOT - ON THE PATH (STOCK)

Slaves carrying heavy chest on their shoulders to f.g.,
others watching - CAMERA MOVES BACK - men drop chest
to open tomb -

           CONTINUED

98	CONTINUED	

        ISMAIL'S VOICE O.S.
    With him was also buried a great
    quantity of the forbidden Tana leaves.

99   SCENE 33 - CLOSE SHOT - ON HILLSIDE (STOCK)

   Priest gives signal as slaves go toward b.g. MUSIC-CHANTING

(* Narrative Missing!)

100 SCENE 34 - MED. CLOSE - ON HILLSIDE (STOCK)
                     MUSIC-CHANTING

   Slaves start to fill the grave -

101 SCENE 36 - CLOSER SHOT - ON HILLSIDE (STOCK)

   Slaves filling in grave in f.g. Priest and soldiers
   beyond - Priest gives signal.

102 SCENE 36 - CLOSE VIEW - LINEUP OF SOLDIERS (STOCK)

   Carrying shields and spears - they raise their spears -
   throw them in unison.

        ISMAIL'S VOICE O.S.
    Then the slaves were killed...

103 SCENE 37 - MED. CLOSE - ON THE HILL   (STOCK)

   The slaves fall - soldiers watch MUSIC-CHANTING

        ISMAIL'S VOICE O.S.
   ...so that they could not tell what
   had taken place.

104 SCENE 38 - CLOSEUP - AT THE PARTLY-FILLED GRAVE (STOCK)

   Bodies of slaves discovered. MUSIC-CHANTING

105 SCENE 39 - MED. CLOSE - ON THE HILLSIDE (STOCK)

   Priest and soldiers standing. MUSIC-CHANTING

             DISSOLVE TO

VIEW ON THE HILLSIDE (STOCK)
Soldiers and slaves pass, carrying the casket of the
Princess - some carrying lighted torches.

               CONTINUED

105   CONTINUED

>   ISMAIL'S VOICE O.S.
>   Later the Priests removed Kharis from
>   his unholy grave and placed him in a
>   cave on the other side of this mountain.

                                              DISSOLVE TO

CLOSEUP - OF THE POOL OF KOR (STOCK)

Vapor swirling and rising from it - CAMERA MOVES BACK from it.

                                              MUSIC-CHANTING

>   ISMAIL'S VOICE O.S.
>   And thus none but the Priests of Karnak
>   know where Kharis had been buried.

                                              DISSOLVE TO

106   INT. MONASTERY - CEREMONIAL ROOM - <u>NIGHT</u> - MED. CLOSE SHOT - ON ISMAIL AND ABBAS

with Mummy case between them. They are standing near the brazier, Ismail leaning over the Mummy case, giving the o.s. Mummy some of the juice. He turns to Abbas.

>   ISMAIL
>   For over three thousand years, Kharis
>   remained there in his cave on the other
>   side of the mountain, waiting to bring
>   death to him who would desecrate Ananka's
>   tomb...for Kharis never really dies...
>
>   ABBAS
>   (looking down at
>   o.s. Mummy in case)
>   Then why, Master, is he here in
>   America?
>
>   ISMAIL
>   (looking about)
>   An American archaeologist, seeking
>   the tomb of Princess Ananka, by
>   accident came upon and dared to
>   desecrate the burial place of Kharis...
>   Because of it, Kharis has reaped a
>   horrible vengeance upon him and all
>   his loved ones...
>
>   ABBAS
>   I know, Master, but once Kharis has
>   had his revenge, why did he not go
>   back to his tomb in Egypt?

                                              CONTINUED

106   CONTINUED

                    ISMAIL
            Kharis desired to carry his Princess
            Ananka back with him, but non-believing
            infidels have driven them into these
            swamps....

                    ABBAS
            That, I have heard....

                    ISMAIL
                (addressing
                 the Mummy)
            Two High Priests of Amon-Ra have
            come to America to bring You and
            Ananka home to Egypt, to repose
            together in eternal and immortal
            peace...

107   CLOSE SHOT - SHOOTING DOWN AT THE MUMMY

        Slowly, his neck begins to pulsate and his head and
        shoulders begin to lift up.

                    ISMAIL'S VOICE O.S.
            Both of these Priests have met
            violent death in the attempt...

        Kharis continues slowly getting up.

108   CLOSE SHOT - ISMAIL AND ABBAS

        in front of Mummy case.

                    ISMAIL
            And now you, ~~Abbas~~ Ragab, shall help me
            to succeed where they have failed...
            We shall fulfill our sacred duty...
            or die by violence in this heathen
            land...

                    ABBAS
                (weakly)
            Yes, Master...

        Suddenly the Mummy rises to full length between them.
        Ismail, noticing, turns.

                    ISMAIL
            You have risen, Kharis...'Tis well...

                                    CONTINUED

108 CONTINUED

Just at this point, the SOUND of a door opening is HEARD. Ismail and Abbas turn in its direction. As the CAMERA TRUCKS BACK, we see this door open, and coming into the Ceremonial Room is a bearded, kindly, patriarchal Sacristan (Sexton) in short white trousers and white shirt, looking almost saintly in these drab and frightening surroundings. Around his waist is a heavy cord, from which dangle many keys. In his hand he holds a lighted torch, with a flame which looks very much like a Crucifix. CAMERA HOLDS ON SACRISTAN as he APPROACHES them.

>   SACRISTAN
>   What does this mean?

Ismail looks at Abbas...he doesn't know the man.

>   ISMAIL
>   (to Sacristan)
>   Who are you? And what are you doing here?

>   SACRISTAN
>   I am ~~Lay Brother~~ Michael...
>   of this Chapel and Monastery...

Noticing the Mummy and other paraphenalia, the Sacristan becomes angry in spite of his kindliness, as he crosses to them.

>   ABBAS
>   We thought this place was abandoned...

>   SACRISTAN
>   This home of Christian worship...
>   though silent for many years...
>   (looks at Mummy)
>   ...is not to be desecrated by such pagan customs...

Ismail looks significantly to the Mummy.

>   SACRISTAN
>   I am afraid I shall have to ask you to take these sacrilegious things away...

Indicates the Mummy, cases and other props.

>   ABBAS
>   (looking to Ismal, obviously stalling)
>   We shall only remain for the night...

CONTINUED

108   CONTINUED - 2

                          SACRISTAN
                 You can not stay here another ~~night~~... hour
                 In a room ---
                          (indicating)
                 ...beyond the Monk cells, I found the
                 bodies of freshly murdered men...
                 Never has this happened, before...

109   CLOSE SHOT - ON ISMAIL

       his head turns in the direction of the Mummy. CAMERA
       PANS WITH HIS LOOK TO THE MUMMY, who steps away from
       the case and starts approaching menacingly toward CAMERA.

110   CLOSE SHOT - ON THE SACRISTAN

       Seeing the o.s. Mummy approach, he holds up his lighted
       torchiere.

                          SACRISTAN
                 I fear you not...So go...

111   CLOSE SHOT - OF REFLECTION OF LIGHT AGAINST WALL

       looking like a flaming cross. CAMERA HOLDS ON THIS
       REFLECTION, and suddenly we HEAR a muffled CRY of pain
       as the reflection of the lighted Cross drops down out
       of SCENE and CAMERA HOLDS ON THE EMPTY WALL a moment,
       as we HEAR the dull thud of the fallen body.

                                                    FADE OUT

       FADE IN

112   EXT. CONSTRUCTION CAMP - DAY - CLOSE SHOT - ON AN OLD
       FASHIONED WATCH - HELD IN GOOBIE'S HAND

       The hands on the watch point to exactly five o'clock.
       Suddenly, we HEAR a BELL TOLL. CAMERA TRUCKS BACK to
       show Goobie holding the watch in one hand as he gives
       it his rapt attention. With the other hand, he pulls at
       a long, hempen rope attached to a bell hanging outside
       Walsh's office. As Goobie continues to pull the rope,
       Abbas COMES INTO SCENE.

                          ABBAS
                 Quitting time already, Goobie?

                          GOOBIE
                          (still pulling rope)
                 Yes, Suh, Mr. Abbas -- five o'clock.

113   MED. LONG SHOT - ON CAMP

   showing men quitting their work, leaving the swamps
   with their lunch pails - coats thrown over their arms.
   OVER SCENE we HEAR GOOBIE'S BELL.

114   EXT. NEAR SWAMP SHORE - DAY - MED. FULL SHOT - ON A WORKMAN

   riding on a bulldozer. GOOBIE'S BELL is HEARD OVER
   SCENE. The workman turns the bulldozer and starts back.

115   MED. LONG SHOT - SHOOTING TOWARD THE BACK OF THE RECEDING
   BULLDOZER

   In f.g., we SEE a peculiar object sticking up out of
   the loose earth uncovered by the bulldozer. It is a
   shriveled, old hand.

116   MED. CLOSE SHOT - ON THE HAND

   Old and shriveled - human, and yet unhuman. The CAMERA
   HOLDS on it as though intrigued, and even cautiously
   MOVES IN CLOSER. As the sunlight of this summer's day
   warms the hand, it actually begins to move a little,
   loosening the earth around it, slowly, at first, then
   picking up tempo as the loosened earth begins to fall
   away from it.

117   MED. SHOT - ON THE BULLDOZER

   making its way toward the shed in b.g.

118   MED. CLOSE SHOT - ON THE HAND AND ARM

   warmed by the sun, it is now strangely youthful, firm
   and strong. As the dirt continues to fall away, the
   aged body of PRINCESS ANANKA is finally revealed - a
   grimy, white-haired, hag-like creature. She tries to
   rise, but falls in the sunlight, with arms outstretched
   toward the sun. She lies there for a moment, CAMERA
   HOLDING on her; then, as if imbued with a new energy
   from the sun's rays, she rises again and starts to wander
   off. She is dressed in the gown she wore when Kharis
   walked into the swamps with her. It is now tattered and
   crusted with earth.

119 MED. SHOT - ON PRINCESS ANANKA

walking toward the swamp, like one in a trance. The TRUCKING CAMERA keeps trailing her, determined not to be shaken off from this phenomenon, until she walks right into a pool or stream of water, emersing herself completely. The CAMERA HOLDS ON THE SPOT, when, wonderful to behold, she comes up with the earthen clay and all vestiges of age and debilities cast off from her, like old clothes. As she turns to face the CAMERA, we see a young girl now - beautiful to face, and with a shapely figure outlined by the wet, clinging and filmy night garment she wore as Amina in THE MUMMY'S GHOST. More intrigued than ever now, the CAMERA STAYS WITH HER as she turns again, and, like a sleepwalker, or one in a trance, starts wandering through the canebrake, holding her arms out yearningly toward the setting sun, and going toward it. Suddenly, from O.S. we HEAR an animal's CRY OF FRIGHT. CAMERA TURNS QUICKLY toward a meadow near the swamp edge where HORSES WHINNY in terror and run; DOGS BARK and slink away. *Not Used!*

120 MED. MOVING SHOT - ON BIG JOE

walking along the swamp edge, lunch pail in hand, his coat slung over his arm. His day's work is done and he is on his way home to his shack, when OVER SCENE he HEARS a continuation of the DOGS BARKING and the HORSES NEIGHING from the previous scene. He turns toward the o.s. dog and calls:

> BIG JOE
> Hey! Pettipas! What'sa ma weet you?
> (imitates dog barking)
> An' you, Marrianne - Cheetah?...

— OMITTED

He neighs like a horse, laughing at himself. Suddenly his laughter dies as he sees something o.s.

121 MED. FULL SHOT - FROM BIG JOE'S ANGLE - ON PRINCESS ANANKA

walking along the swamp edge toward the setting sun.

122 MED. CLOSE SHOT - ON BIG JOE

looking with surprise at this strange creature approaching from b.g. His look of surprise gives way to one of extreme pleasure as he notices her beauty of face and form. CAMERA TRUCKS IN to a CLOSER SHOT as Princess Ananka draws near to Big Joe, still walking as though in a trance.

CONTINUED

122   CONTINUED

                    BIG JOE
          Hello....I no see you before...
          Where you come from?

     Princess Ananka continues as if she neither sees nor
     hears him. Coming closer, Big Joe takes another look
     at her and suddenly realizes the girl is in a trance.

123   CLOSE SHOT - FROM BIG JOE'S ANGLE - ON PRINCESS ANANKA

     She has a vague look on her face. Her clothes are still
     wet, clinging close to her body. She seems completely
     unconscious of Big Joe and her surroundings.

124   CLOSE TWO SHOT - ON BIG JOE AND PRINCESS ANANKA

     as Big Joe stops her.

                    BIG JOE
          Hey...you wet...Better take my
          coat.

     He takes his coat and puts it around her shoulders.

                    BIG JOE
          I theenk somethin' happen to you,
          huh?

     When she doesn't respond, Big Joe is at a complete loss,
     not knowing what to make of the girl, or what to do with
     her.

                    BIG JOE
                 (with sudden thought)
          You come with me.

                    PRINCESS ANANKA
                 (without expression)
          Kharis..

125   MED. SHOT - AT PATHWAY NEAR SWAMP EDGE

     Abbas, on his way to the monastery after the day's work
     is done, suddenly stops as he HEARS O.S. VOICES.

                    BIG JOE'S VOICE O.S.
          Kharis?

     Abbas reacts with a start, then turns and sees Ananka
     and Big Joe approaching from o.s. He steps back in the
     shrubbery to conceal himself.

126   MED. CLOSE TRUCKING SHOT - ON BIG JOE AND PRINCESS
      ANANKA

                    BIG JOE
          What is this Kharis? Maybe that
          your name?

Ananka still does not answer as they walk INTO SCENE
where Abbas is concealed in shrubbery in b.g.

                    BIG JOE
          Come on. I tak' you to Tante
          Berthe.

As they walk past CAMERA, OUT OF SCENE, Abbas steps
out of his place on concealment and watches after them.

                    BIG JOE'S VOICE O.S.
          She feex you up awright.

Abbas watches o.s. for a moment longer, then darts into
the shrubbery as if taking the shortest possible way to
the monastery to tell Ismail. CAMERA PANS with him.

*- Continuation On Page 44   DISSOLVE

127   INT. MONASTERY - CEREMONIAL ROOM - <u>NIGHT</u> - CLOSE SHOT -
      ON TANA LEAVES BREWING

CAMERA TRUCKS BACK, DISCLOSING that we are in the
interior of the monastery. Ismail is brewing the
magic potion.

                    ISMAIL
                (without looking up)
          Is Kharis ready?   } OMIT

                    ABBAS VOICE O.S.
          Yes, Master...

                    ISMAIL
          Then let him approach.

CAMERA TRUCKS BACK to a WIDER ANGLE as Abbas and the
Mummy come forward.

*- Begin From Page 47
                    ISMAIL
                (to Mummy)
          The hour has come, Kharis...the
          moment for which you have waited
          so long. Abbas has seen the
          Princess Ananka, your bride, taken
          to Tante Berthe's Cafe.

                                        CONTINUED

vk   "THE MUMMY'S RETURN" - 7/7/44   44

127   CONTINUED

        Ismail hands the vessel with the potent liquid to the
        Mummy who turns his back and starts to drink it.

                            ISMAIL
                Yes, drink... drink from the brew
                of the Nine Tana leaves.

        Having taken his fill of it, the Mummy hands the vessel
        to Abbas, then turns toward Ismail.

        Some dialogue missing
                            ISMAIL
                Now you shall go to take her...
                and any who would stand in your
                way... kill.... kill...

        * Return to Page 47

128   MED. FULL SHOT

        The Mummy starts on his quest, shuffling his way OUT OF
        THE ROOM. Ismail watches after him, then turns with a
        look toward Abbas. Abbas hurries after the Mummy.

                                                    WIPE TO

129   EXT. MONASTERY STEPS - NIGHT - MED. FULL PAN SHOT -
        ON THE MUMMY AND ABBAS

        making their way down the steps, the Mummy in the lead.
        CAMERA PANS with them. The Mummy EXITS SCENE as Abbas
        halts in f.g., on lower step, and watches him go.

                                                    DISSOLVE

        *— From Page 43 - START HERE!

130   EXT. TANTE BERTHE'S CAJUN CAFE - NIGHT - MED. FULL SHOT

        From within, we HEAR the SOUND OF MUSIC and TANTE BERTHE
        SINGING. The place is brightly lit as Big Joe and
        Princess Ananka approach. Ananka still wears Big Joe's
        coat. Instead of being indifferent to him, she now
        clings closely to Big Joe and seems eager to go with him
        into the cafe. Big Joe senses this as they halt at corner
        of building in f.g.

                            BIG JOE
                We don' go in thees way... we go
                roun' back to Tante Berthe.

        Big Joe leads the way around corner of cafe.

131   EXT. REAR OF TANTE BERTHE'S CAFE - NIGHT - MED. SHOT -
        ON BIG JOE AND ANANKA

        Joe leads the girl around corner and up to door. SOUND
        OF SINGING AND MUSIC is HEARD from o.s. Joe knocks.
        There is no answer. He knocks again, then opens the door
        and ENTERS with Ananka.

132   INT. TANTE BERTHE'S BEDROOM - NIGHT - MED. SHOT - ON
        BIG JOE AND ANANKA

        who still moves as though she is in a trance - as they
        come in through rear door. The room is unoccupied, but
        SOUND OF MUSIC and TANTE BERTHE SINGING is heard from
        cafe proper. The room is distinctively furnished in
        the attractive provencal Cajun period. Every bit of wall
        space is covered with family pictures and framed mementos,
        in typical French manner. In the center of the room is a
        large four-posted bed. Big Joe glances about somewhat
        ill-at-ease, then places Ananka on the bed.

                        BIG JOE
              You wait here... I fin' Tante
              Berthe.

        Ananka pays no attention to this but glances slowly about
        the room as Joe crosses to the door leading into the cafe
        and opens it. MUSIC AND TANTE BERTHE'S SINGING INCREASES.

133   INT. TANTE BERTHE'S CAFE - NIGHT - CLOSE SHOT - ON BIG JOE

        as he opens door from bedroom and glances out.

134   MED. FULL SHOT - FROM BIG JOE'S ANGLE - ON A GROUP OF
        HAPPY-GO-LUCKY CAJUNS

        gathered about Tante Berthe who is just finishing her
        song, accompanying herself on the accordian. Ulysses is
        nearby, watching her with a proud smile. The SONG ENDS
        and the Cajuns applaud and cheer for more.

135   MED. CLOSE SHOT - ON TANTE BERTHE, ULYSSES AND A FEW
        CAJUNS - OVERLAPPING ACTION OF THE ABOVE SCENE

        Tante Berthe is about to comply with the ad lib requests
        for another song when she happens to glance off toward
        the bedroom.

136   MED. SHOT - FROM TANTE BERTHE'S ANGLE - ON BIG JOE

standing in the partly-open bedroom door. He motions silently for Tante Berthe to join him, then steps back into the bedroom and closes the door.

137   MED. CLOSE SHOT - ON TANTE BERTHE, ULYSSES AND CAJUNS

Tante Berthe reacts in amazement to Big Joe's presence in her bedroom, then quickly gives her accordian to Ulysses and speaks laughingly:

> TANTE BERTHE
> I seeng for you 'gain after 'while, mebbe.

Tante Berthe slaps a couple of the Cajuns on the back as Ulysses begins playing the accordian and the Cajuns start singing. Tante Berthe crosses to the bedroom door, CAMERA PANNING with her.

138   INT. TANTE BERTHE'S BEDROOM - NIGHT - MED. CLOSE SHOT - ON BIG JOE

waiting near the door. He steps back quickly as the door opens and Tante Berthe HURRIES IN. Big Joe quickly closes the door after her.

> TANTE BERTHE
> (severely)
> What you do here in my room, Big Joe?!

Big Joe puts his fingers to his lips for silence, then nods off toward Princess Ananka o.s. Tante Berthe stares in that direction in amazement, then slowly follows Big Joe across the room. CAMERA DOLLIES ALONG with them to a MED. CLOSE SHOT, TAKING IN Ananka on the bed, apparently still in a trance.

> BIG JOE
> I fin' dees poor girl in swamp. She ees ver' seeck.

Tante Berthe moves forward and takes Ananka's hand, then whirls on Big Joe. *NARATIVE MISSING*

> TANTE BERTHE
> Why you stan' there? You breeng company doctor, no?

> BIG JOE
> (hurriedly)
> Awright - awright -- you tak' good care from her.

CONTINUED

138   CONTINUED

                    TANTE BERTHE
          You no worry 'bout dat.. Queeck go..
          M'sieur Le Medicin get...

     Big Joe nods and EXITS FROM SCENE toward rear door.

139   MED. SHOT - OVERLAPPING ACTION OF THE ABOVE SCENE

     Big Joe crosses to rear door, then halts a moment and
     looks sympathetically back at Ananka, as Tante Berthe
     speaks to the girl.

                    TANTE BERTHE
          I feex bed for you -- den you
          rest.

     Tante Berthe starts to arrange the bed as Big Joe goes
     out the door.

     *– Return to Page 43!

140   EXT. REAR OF TANTE BERTHE'S CAFE - NIGHT - MED. SHOT -
       ON BIG JOE * From Page 44

     as he comes out of rear door of cafe, then hurries away
     at angle into the swamp, CAMERA PANNING with him. As he
     disappears from view, CAMERA SWINGS abruptly over to a
     picturesque spot among shrubs and trees to PICK UP the
     distant silhouetted figure of the Mummy, moving slowly
     through the shadows toward Camera.

141   EXT. NEAR REAR OF TANTE BERTHE'S CAFE - NIGHT - MED.
       PAN SHOT - ON THE MUMMY

     moving methodically along shrubbery. The SOUND OF REVELRY
     and MUSIC from the cafe is heard faintly from o.s.

142   INT. TANTE BERTHE'S BEDROOM - NIGHT - MED. CLOSE SHOT -
       ON TANTE BERTHE AND ANANKA - AT BED

     Tante Berthe is adjusting the covers over the still
     trance-like Ananka; then she speaks solicitously:

                    TANTE BERTHE
          You feel maybe perhap bettaire,
          no?

     Ananka turns slowly, a fiant smile on her face as she
     glances up at Tante Berthe. Suddenly she tenses and her
     eyes widen as she stares off toward the side window.

143   MED. CLOSE SHOT - ON WINDOW

We see the grotesque figure of the Mummy halt at the window a moment, then EXIT from scene toward door.

144   MED. SHOT - SHOOTING TOWARD REAR DOOR - TAKING IN TANTE BERTHE AND ANANKA AT BED

Tante Berthe notices the girl's fearful expression. As she glances up, her eyes widen fearfully as the methodical footsteps halt outside the door. Then the door opens and the Mummy appears inside the opening.

145   MED. CLOSE SHOT - REVERSE ANGLE - SHOOTING PAST THE MUMMY TOWARD BED IN B.G.

As the Mummy moves slowly but menacingly forward, and CAMERA DOLLIES along with it, Ananka leaps from the bed and dashes across the room. The Mummy turns to grab her but Tante Berthe jumps from the bed and moves protectingly between them. Closer and closer the Mummy moves toward Tante Berthe who tries to scream, but fear convulses her throat and no sound comes out.

146   CLOSE SHOT - LOW ANGLE - SHOOTING UP ACROSS BED - OPEN DOOR B.G.

The Mummy, with outstreched hand, stoops down to press Tante Berthe OUT OF PICTURE. Above the SOUND of the MUSIC IN THE CAFE, we HEAR a GASP, and in b.g. we see Ananka, wraith-like, fly past the Mummy and escape by the open door in b.g.

147   MED. SHOT - OVERLAPPING ACTION OF THE ABOVE SCENE

The Mummy turns, releasing his hold on Tante Berthe who falls to the floor behind the bed. Then the Mummy Ominously EXITS through rear door after Ananka.

148   EXT. REAR OF TANTE BERTHE'S CAFE - <u>NIGHT</u> - MED. FULL SHOT SHOOTING PAST REAR OF CAFE

In f.g. we see Ananka running fearfully away from the cafe. As she EXITS past Camera, the Mummy COMES THROUGH open rear door and moves methodically but ominously OUT OF SCENE after her.

149   EXT. NEAR REAR OF TANTE BERTHE'S CAFE - <u>NIGHT</u> - MED.
      FULL SHOT - ON PRINCESS ANANKA

      as she runs fearfully INTO SCENE past Camera, and halting,
      glances back.

150   MED. FULL SHOT - FROM HER ANGLE - ON THE MUMMY

      as he makes his way INTO SCENE among trees, halts a
      moment till he spots the girl, then moves menacingly on
      OUT OF SCENE past Camera.

151   MED. SHOT - ON ANANKA

      as she reacts to the Mummy's pursuit of her, glances
      fearfully about, then turns and runs on - among trees
      in b.g.

152   MED. FULL SHOT - OVERLAPPING ACTION OF THE ABOVE SCENE

      as Ananka runs hurriedly into trees in b.g. and DISAPPEARS.
      The Mummy comes INTO SCENE past Camera and plods
      menacingly on after her.

                                              DISSOLVE

153   EXT. SWAMP - <u>NIGHT</u> - MED. FULL SHOT - ON ANANKA

      making her way through the swamp toward Camera. She
      halts in f.g. and glances back as we HEAR a SPLASHING
      SOUND O.S.

154   MED. SHOT - FROM ANANKA'S ANGLE - ON THE MUMMY

      as he comes INTO SCENE through swamp, splashing through
      the mud and water.

155   MED. FULL SHOT - ON ANANKA

      In b.g., we SEE the Mummy come INTO SCENE, stalking
      methodically closer to her. The girl turns and hurries
      frantically away through the swamp - the Mummy still in
      pursuit. CAMERA PANS with Ananka as she reaches a firm
      footing on the road, and glancing back, turns and runs
      wearily on down the road into the night.

156   EXT. ROAD - NIGHT - MED. SHOT ON ANANKA

as she runs along road toward CAMERA, then suddenly halts as the SOUND of a CAR APPROACHING O.S. IS HEARD. The lights from the car strike her. She is blinded for a moment, then turns and runs toward the approaching headlights.

157   MED. FULL PAN SHOT - ON ANANKA

running along the road toward the approaching headlights of the car. The car roars INTO SCENE, driver by Halsey, with Betty in the seat beside him. Halsey slams on the brakes in the nick of time as the car screeches to a halt, barely missing Ananka. Ananka collapses to the road.

158   MED. SHOT - ON HALSEY AND BETTY - IN CAR - OVERLAPPING ACTION OF ABOVE SCENE

They react to seeing the strange girl collapse in front of them and Halsey quickly opens the door. Both get out and cross to the girl in the road, CAMERA PANNING with them.

    BETTY
   (frightened)
 I thought sure we were going to
 hit her.

    HALSEY
 She must have fainted -- from the
 scare.

Both kneel beside the girl and CAMERA DOLLIES INTO CLOSE SHOT. Betty eyes Ananka's flimsy, tattered dress, and remarks in amazement:

    BETTY
 Look at the way she's dressed --
 Strange clothes to be wearing out
 in the swamp at this hour of the
 night.

Halsey nods, and begins to make a quick examination of Ananka to see if she's hurt.

159   EXT. SWAMP - NIGHT - MED. TRAVEL SHOT - ON THE MUMMY

as he makes his way from the swampland toward the road. He halts and glances off toward the road and car o.s., then moves ominously OUT OF SCENE in that direction.

re

160   EXT. ROAD - <u>NIGHT</u> - MED. SHOT - ON BETTY & HALSEY

completing their examination of the unconscious Ananka who is still lying on the road, Betty's coat tucked around her.

> HALSEY
> So far as I can hastily guess, Betty, she's only suffering from shock and exhaustion. We'd bettter get her back to camp at once, and have Dr. Cooper take care of her.

Betty nods and Halsey bends down and picks the girl up in his arms, leaving the coat on the ground. They get to their feet and CAMERA PANS THEM to the car. Betty opens the door of the car while Halsey tries to put Ananka inside.

161   MED. CLOSE SHOT - SHOOTING THROUGH WINDOW OF CAR TOWARDS SWAMP IN B.G.

Halsey places Ananka in the back seat of the car, while Betty helps. In b.g., we see the Mummy come out of the swamp toward the road and move ominously toward the car. Halsey takes blankets from the car and wraps them around the girl and then closes the door.

162   MED. CLOSE SHOT - REVERSE ANGLE

overlapping action of the above SCENE. Betty and Halsey start to climb into the front of the car. Then Betty suddenly glances down the road.

> BETTY
> My coat -- We left it in the road back there.   } NOT SAID!
>
> HALSEY
> I'll get it.

Halsey turns and EXITS toward the road where the coat has been left.

163   MED. FULL SHOT - ON SECTION OF ROAD WHERE COAT IS LYING

Halsey ENTERS to coat and as he picks it up, we see Mummy move ominously to SCENE, PAST CAMERA. He halts a moment and then, as Halsey turns and walks back to the car and starts to get into the driver's seat, the Mummy moves forward without their observing him. He reaches out, as though to grab the car, then Halsey shifts gears and the automobile pulls OUT OF SCENE, CAMERA PANNING with it.

re

164 MED. SHOT - ON THE MUMMY

as he stares after the car. Then turning, he plunges away from the road, into the swampland, CAMERA PANNING WITH HIM.

                                        DISSOLVE

165 EXT. REAR OF TANTE BERTHE'S CAFE - <u>NIGHT</u> - MED. FULL SHOT - ON A SMALL COUPE

as it drives up to rear of Cafe and halts. Dr. Cooper and Big Joe get out and cross to rear door which is open.

166 INT. TANTE BERTHE'S BEDROOM - <u>NIGHT</u> - MED. CLOSE SHOT - SHOOTING TOWARD DOORWAY

Big Joe ENTERS with Dr. Cooper, and both halt in amazement as they stare ahead. OVER SCENE we HEAR the SOUNDS OF WEEPING and muffled, awed voices. CAMERA TRUCKS BACK to reveal Tante Berthe is sprawled on the bed. Ulysses is down on his knees, his head in his arms, leaning on the bed, weeping convulsively. Crowded in the open doorway, whispering among themselves in hushed and awesome tones, are the natives, who, only a moment ago were singing so gayly.

> BIG JOE
> (calling out excitedly)
> What'sa ma here?

Big Joe leads the way for the Doctor and he forces a path through the crowded group.

> BIG JOE (cont'd)
> What 'appen?
> (with great anxiety)
> Where the girl?....

The question goes unanswered. Ulysses is too steeped in grief to respond.

> CAJUN GIRL
> (to Halsey)
> We all hav' good time singing
> Fais dodo...Ulysses come in here --
> and Tante Berthe she on bed...

The Doctor immediately crosses to bed to examine Tante Berthe.

167   MED. CLOSE GROUP SHOT - NATIVES

crowded in doorway, stand by in a hushed silence that is
intensified by Ulysses's sobs.

>   DR. COOPER
>   (o.s.)
>   This woman's dead....

Even though the natives suspected as much temselves, this
confirmation of their fears, coming from the Doctor has
a tremendous, frightening effect on them.

>   DR. COOPER (cont'd)
>   (o.s.)
>   Death by strangulation...

168   CLOSE GROUP SHOT - NEAR THE BED

Big Joe crosses to Ulysses and pats his shoulder in warm,
heartfelt sympathy. Then he leans over the body, o.s.

>   BIG JOE
>   (to Doctor, excitedly)
>   Whassa funny marks on the throat?...
>   Looks mebbe lak mold ---

>   DR. COOPER
>   (looking)
>   Quite so.. Odd, isn't it?

>   BIG JOE
>   Poor Tante Berthe... She'sa dead...
>   and the girl, she'sa gone... What
>   'appen to her?

As Dr. Cooper turns to look at him, completely baffled
by the unexpected turn of events, Big Joe moves to the
sorrowful Ulysses and tries to comfort him.

                                           FADE OUT

FADE IN

169 EXT. ENTRANCE TO BETTY'S TENT - DAY - MED. CLOSE SHOT

Walsh ENTERS SCENE, followed by Big Joe.

> WALSH *Following omitted*
> (calling)
> Betty!
> (then a little louder
> and more impatient)
> Betty!!!!

> BETTY
> (coming out; trying
> to quiet him)
> Shhhh!...shhh!

She leads the two men away from the entrance of tent, CAMERA PANS WITH THEM.

> WALSH
> (impatiently)
> What's going on here?

> BETTY
> Dr. Cooper's inside with that girl...

170 CLOSE SHOT - ON WALSH

> WALSH
> (irritated)
> Will you tell me what I'm running... an Engineering Company, or a charity hospital?

> BETTY
> Please, Uncle Pat...

171 GROUP SHOT - BETTY, WALSH AND BIG JOE

> BIG JOE
> You theenk maybe perhap' Miss Walsh, I might talk to her...

He indicates.

> BETTY
> Oh, not now... while the Doctor's there....

> BIG JOE
> I bring her to Tante Berthe.... and Berthe is killed...with funny marks on her throat. Maybe this girl she can tell us something....

CONTINUED

171   CONTINUED

> BETTY
> You couldn't talk to her now...
> I don't think the doctor would
> allow it,...

> WALSH
> (now aggravated)
> Will you forget about this girl...
> and let's get down to business.
> I need you over at the office...
> I've got to have somebody there
> who knows how to manage....

> BETTY
> Just as soon as I talk to Dr. Cooper,
> I promise you I'll be right over...

> WALSH
> (cutting in; dolefully)
> I should have known better than
> to let that college professor
> and his...

> BETTY
> He had nothing to do with this,
> Uncle Pat... so don't blame him...

Just at this point Halsey ENTERS THE SCENE brightly.

> HALSEY
> Good morning, Betty...Morning
> Mr. Walsh... Big Joe....

> BETTY
> (sweetly)
> Good morning...

> WALSH
> (takes one look)
> He had nothing to do with it,
> huh?
> (disgustedly)
> Come on, Joe.

He EXITS.

> BIG JOE
> Maybe see her later...Yes?

He shrugs and EXITS.

> HALSEY
> (looking toward tent)
> How is she?

CONTINUED

171   CONTINUED - 2

                    BETTY
          Dr. Cooper just says she's ill
          and suffering from exposure...
          Frankly, I think he's just as
          puzzled as we are...

From o.s. we HEAR

                    DR. COOPER'S VOICE
                         (calling)
          Miss Walsh!

They turn, CAMERA PANS WITH THEM TO THE TENT ENTRANCE, as the doctor comes out.

172   CLOSE GROUP SHOT - BETTY, HALSEY, DR. COOPER

                    DR. COOPER
          Until such time as I can find
          accomodations for her at the
          camp infirmary, do you think
          the young lady could remain here
          in your tent?

                    BETTY
          Of course, Doctor...
                         (little nervously)
          The only thing is, I can't be
          with her all the time... I have
          work waiting at the office....

[↑ OMITTED]

                    DR. COOPER
          All she needs is rest and
          nourishment....

Just at this moment they HEAR coming from the tent Ananka's stifled scream.

                    ANANKA'S VOICE   [Begin Here!]
                         (stifled scream)

The three look at each other, then RUSH into the tent.

173   INT. BETTY'S TENT - <u>DAY</u> - MED. CLOSE SHOT - ON ANANKA

sitting up on the cot. Her face is terrified. Betty, Halsey and Dr. Cooper rush in.

                    ANANKA
          What has happened to me?.....I woke
          up -- and everything was so strange --

174   CLOSE SHOT - ON ANANKA

She looks around. We see there is not the slightest bit of recognition in her expression as her attention goes from one to the other.

>   ANANKA
>   (almost imploringly)
>   Who are you?

175   MED. GROUP SHOT - HALSEY, BETTY, DR. COOPER AND ANANKA

as the Doctor approaches her.

>   DR. COOPER
>   We're friends who found you
>   wandering on the road....

The girl reacts, as though it were hard for her to believe.

>   ANANKA
>   Wandering on the road?

>   DR. COOPER
>   Dr. Halsey, Miss Walsh and I
>   brought you here...

>   BETTY
>   (sincerely concerned)
>   Are you feeling better?

>   ANANKA
>   (now pathetically
>   shaking her head)
>   I can't remember...who I am...
>   O what I'm doing here...

>   HALSEY
>   Big Joe found you earlier and
>   brought you to Tante Berthe...the
>   Cajun woman...Do you remember that?

>   ANANKA
>   (repeating)
>   Tante Berthe... Cajun woman?

She shakes her head.

>   DR. COOPER
>   You've probably suffered a severe shock...
>   There's nothing to fear...just rest quietly
>   and you'll be all right...

Dr. Cooper beckons to Halsey and Betty and they start following him OUT.

                                                  CONTINUED

175   CONTINUED

>   DR. COOPER (cont'd)
>   (turning back to girl)
>   I'll drop in to see how you are later...

The girl doesn't respond.

176   EXT. TENT ENTRANCE - **DAY** - MED. CLOSE SHOT

Betty and Halsey COME OUT. They look at one another, then questioningly turn to Dr. Cooper.

>   DR. COOPER
>   The poor girl is definitely a victim
>   of amnesia. Give her something to do --
>   something to keep her mentally alert...
>   and talking as much as possible.
>   (after a pause)
>   Your Laboratory might be just the place...
>
>   HALSEY
>   I'll start her in the morning -- another
>   day's rest won't hurt her.

                                        DISSOLVE

177   EXT. HALSEY'S LABORATORY TENT - WIDE ANGLE - **DAY** - MED. SHOT

Ananka seated at a small desk, upon which is piled a number of research books and many old Egyptian Vases and pottery fragments, all pushed aside to make way for microscope and a series of slides. Behind her, the tent flap above the side wall is rolled. The sun pours down upon her and the desk, flooding everything with a glaring light. She is wearing a very attractive frock of Betty's and anyone seeing her, thus engaged, would never suspect that there was anything wrong with the girl. She is at the moment looking into the microscope, quickly making notations on a pad beside her, when Halsey ENTERS through the tent entrance. He sees her there in the glaring sun, stops in surprise and calls:

>   HALSEY
>   (cheerfully)
>   Hello...What are you trying to do...
>   develope a fine case of sun-stroke?
>
>   ANANKA
>   (looking up)
>
>   Oh, good morning, Dr. Halsey...
>   I hope you don't mind me working
>   out here... I had one of the men
>   move the desk. I love the sun....

                                        CONTINUED

177 CONTINUED

> HALSEY
> O.K. ... but does it love you that much? Or will you be shining like a boiled crawfish in an hour or two?

> ANANKA
> (smiling sweetly to him) — *Dialogue Missing!*
> I can never get too much of the sun... By the way, if you'll excuse my saying so... I think you're wrong about this Mummy cloth...

Halsey crosses up to her, rather amused.

> HALSEY
> You do, huh?

CAMERA TRUCKS IN TO A CLOSE SHOT OF HALSEY AND THE GIRL

He stands by desk where she is seated.

> ANANKA
> This cloth is not part of the Mummy wrappings of Kharis...

He looks down at her quickly, completely surprised - his mouth opens wide...this is something he never expected.

> ANANKA (cont'd)
> (rises and steps away from chair)
> See for yourself, Doctor Halsey..

Halsey sits down - looks in microscope.

> ANANKA (cont'd)
> Notice the lacy net-work of the linen strands.. If you count them you will find that they number more than three hundred and forty-four to the square inch, making a fine soft tightly woven material - almost silk-like...

Halsey looks up at her amazed as she continues.

> ANANKA (cont'd)
> No, Doctor, a man's cloth would be more loosely woven and of coarser material.

He looks back into microscope.

CONTINUED

177   CONTINUED - 2

> ANANKA (cont'd)
> This is the fabric in which a
> woman might be wrapped...

[margin note: No Mention of Princess ANAN KA Only Khanis!]

Halsey looks up again, almost startled.

> HALSEY
> Did you say a woman?

> ANANKA
> Yes, Doctor Halsey....
>   (glibly, almost
>   mechanically)
> I'd say a woman of royal blood...
> of the Dynasty of King Amenophis...
> In fact, this piece was part of the
> shroud of the King's own daughter..
> the Princess Ananka...

Halsey gets up, stares at the girl.

> HALSEY
> How do you know all that?

> ANANKA
>   (completely at a
>   loss to explain)
> I don't know how....

[margin note: Dialogue missing!]

She puts her hand to her mouth as though unaware of what she has been saying. Halsey suddenly realizes, in spite of all doubt, this girl is potentially the source of much valuable information.

> HALSEY
> Say.. if you're right... this
> is terrific...

Before he can finish she crosses by him, as though suddenly in a trance again and starts walking away. THE CAMERA PANS WITH HER and we see she is walking toward Ismail, who has made a silent entrance into the scene, CAMERA TRUCKING BACK TO WIDER ANGLE, taking in all three. Halsey, now completely thrown off, follows after her, the CAMERA TRUCKING IN TO A CLOSER SHOT of the group. The girl continues approaching Ismail with complete lack on inhibition, as though unaccountably drawn to him.

178   CLOSE SHOT - ISMAIL - SHOOTING OVER ANANKA'S SHOULDER

As she approaches he looks at her and then, as though inexplicably frightened by her actions, attempts to draw away. She, however, continues to come closer, as if expecting him to take her in his arms, or carry her away, or... something. A peculiar expression lights his inscrutable face. He bows to her, most humbly, as if she were indeed a royal personage.

179 CLOSE SHOT - FROM A REVERSE ANGLE - HALSEY - WITH ANANKA AND ISMAIL SILHOUETTED IN THE F.G.

> HALSEY
> Ismail...Do you know this young lady?

180 CLOSE GROUP SHOT - CENTERING ON ISMAIL

> ISMAIL
> (smiles blandly)
> No, sir...

Then, as though terribly embarrassed, he turns and hurries OUT OF SCENE. As he does, Ananka goes after him.

> HALSEY
> (seeing this; calls)
> Ismail...Just a minute...

181 EXT. CAMP - NEAR LABORATORY TENT - DAY - MED. SHOT

Ismail is walking toward his tent, looking back over so cautiously, giving the impression that possibly he is trying to lead Ananka away. And the girl follows... until Halsey, hurrying out of the tent, catches up to her, and stops her, by taking her arm. Ismail quickly disappears in his tent.

182 CLOSE SHOT - ON HALSEY AND ANANKA

Halsey excitedly turns her around - Ananka now is in a trance-like state again, and she mumbles...

> ANANKA
> Kharis...Kharis...

Halsey's grasp on her arms tightens.. Before he realizes it he is shaking her.

> HALSEY
> What are you saying?

In fact, he shakes her so violently that the girl suddenly snaps out of it.

> ANANKA
> I'm sorry...I don't know what possessed me...I...

> HALSEY
> What did you mean by calling Kharis?

He is still holding her by the shoulders.

CONTINUED

182 CONTINUED

> ANANKA
> Did I?

> HALSEY
> (as he looks at
> at her sharply)
> Don't you know who Kharis is?

> ANANKA
> (guilelessly)
> No...

Just at this moment from o.s. we HEAR:

> BETTY'S VOICE
> Good morning... *— Following Not Included ↓

CAMERA TRUCKS BACK TO WIDER ANGLE as Betty ENETRS THE SCENE. Halsey, unaware of it, is still holding Ananka by the shoulders close to him. Betty's eyes wander from the girl to Halsey and back again...Getting no immediate response, she calls to them.

> BETTY
> (meaningly)
> I hope I'm not intruding...

For the first time Halsey realizes his position.

> HALSEY
> (quickly dropping
> his hands)
> Our young friend here has had another...
> (gropes for a word)
> spell...

Strangely Betty is not too sympathetic...there may be indications of jealousy.

> BETTY
> That's too bad...

> ANANKA
> Please forgive me, I can't understand...

> HALSEY
> (to Betty)
> Would you mind taking her over to Dr. Cooper?...

Betty, seeing Ananka is actually nervously unstrung, softens.

> BETTY
> Yes, I'll be glad to...

CONTINUED

182   CONTINUED - 2

>   ANANKA
>   (to Betty)
>   No thanks...But if you have no
>   objection, I would rather go back
>   to the tent with you...I...
>
>   BETTY
>   If you need medical attention,
>   Dr. Cooper....
>
>   ANANKA
>   (cutting politely)
>   No...I'm all right, really...
>   It's just that I'm tired and
>   need a little rest...
>
>   BETTY
>   (starting toward tent)
>   Whatever you say...
>
>   HALSEY
>   See you later, Betty...

He watches the two EXIT FROM SCENE. CAMERA MOVES IN TO
A CLOSE SHOT OF HALSEY. He stands there, unable to
figure out this strange creature... her mysterious movements, her sudden attraction for Ismail... And it all
doesn't seem to add up to anything but...perplexity.

                                                FADE OUT

FADE IN   ✘ **Begin Next Scene Here!**

183   EXT. MONASTERY STEPS - <u>NIGHT</u> - FULL SHOT

Ismail in his priestly garment, comes down steps with
Kharis, and halts near top.

184   MED. SHOT - ON THE TWO

>   ISMAIL
>   (looks heavenward)
>   It is the will of Amon-Ra, Kharis...
>   This morning I might have led the Princess
>   Ananka to <u>you</u>...had not Dr. Halsey inter-
>   fered. But it has been ordained that you
>   must seek her out, yourself...

Ismail holds his hand up over the Mummy as though
blessing him.

                                                CONTINUED

184 CONTINUED

ISMAIL (cont'd)
Hasten then... While the moon is high...

The Mummy starts down the long Temple steps, CAMERA PANNING WITH HIM, as he disappears from view.

185 LONG SHOT - SHOOTING UP THE LONG TEMPLE STEPS

showing the Mummy shuffling his way down. His figure looms monstrous and forbidding as he EXITS into brush, CAMERA PANNING WITH HIM.

DISSOLVE TO

186 EXT. CONSTRUCTION CAMP - NIGHT - MED. FULL SHOT - ON CAMP

It is in darkness save for a light in the camp infirmary at the edge of a tree-shaded path.

187 INT. BETTY'S TENT - NIGHT - MED. SHOT - ON ANANKA

lying on a cot in the tent which is lighted only by streaks of moonlight from outside. Across from her, on another cot is Betty, asleep. Ananka, who is tossing restlessly, suddenly sits up, frightened, as she hears the faint SOUND of methodically shuffling footsteps and the cracking of twigs from outside. Quickly, she slips on a white robe and hurries out of the tent.

188 EXT. CONSTRUCTION CAMP - NIGHT - MED. CLOSE SHOT - ON ANANKA

as she goes outside tent, glancing apprehensively off in direction of shuffling footsteps which are HEARD approaching o.s.

189 MED. FULL SHOT - FROM HER ANGLE - ON THE MUMMY

as it comes into view among the trees at one side of camp, halting a moment, moves ominously onward in the direction of Betty's tent.

190 MED. CLOSE SHOT - ON ANANKA

She reacts with fear at the sight of the Mummy, then glancing quickly about, whirls and runs OUT OF SCENE toward infirmary tent, CAMERA PANNING WITH HER as she turns and heads toward tent in b.g. which is lighted.

191   MED. FULL SHOT - REVERSE ANGLE

taking in infirmary tent in b.g. and the girl running toward it. In the f.g. the Mummy appears, then lumbers on through the camp in pursuit of Ananka.

192   MED. CLOSE TRAVEL SHOT - ON ANANKA

running toward infirmary, her hair loosely falling to her shoulders. She glances back toward Mummy o.s., then continues on.

193   MED. TRAVEL SHOT - ON MUMMY

moving ominously along through the camp, after the girl.

194   MED. SHOT - ON ANANKA

as she rushes up to the front of the infirmary tent which is lighted and glances apprehensively back, then hurries inside.

195   INT. INFIRMARY TENT - MED. SHOT - ON TENT

which is a combination Doctor's office with two or three hospital cots in evidence. Dr. Cooper, pipe in his mouth and wearing a doctor's gown and carpet slippers, is seated at his desk reading, when Ananka hurries inside. The doctor gets to his feet in amazement as the girl confronts him. CAMERA DOLLIES INTO A CLOSE TWO SHOT.

       ANANKA
  Pardon me for breaking in like this,
  Doctor -- but I need your help.
    (then imploringly)
  I need help desperately.

       DR. COOPER
    (quietly)
  I'm afraid no one will be able to
  help you -- in the state you're in.
    (then indicating
     a chair)
  Sit down.

Ananka shakes her head and speaks in tremulous half-whisper.

       ANANKA
  He's coming for me.

CONTINUED

195 CONTINUED

>   DR. COOPER
>   (puzzled)
>   Who's coming for you?

>   ANANKA
>   Kharis.

>   DR. COOPER
>   Who's Kharis?

196 CLOSEUP - ON ANANKA

>   ANANKA
>   I don't know.
>   (then almost
>   hysterically)
>   It's so hard to explain. It is
>   as though I were two different
>   people. Sometimes it seems as if
>   I belong to a different world -- I
>   find myself in strange surroundings
>   with strange people. I can't ever
>   seem to find rest, and now Kharis --

197 CLOSEUP - ON THE DOCTOR - OVERLAPPING DIALOGUE IN ABOVE SCENE

He eyes the girl closely, then speaks gently.

>   DR. COOPER
>   You wait here. I'll get you something
>   to quiet your nerves.

198 MED. CLOSE SHOT - ON THE TWO

The Doctor turns to leave. Ananka grabs his arm.

>   ANANKA
>   (imploringly)
>   Please don't go -- don't leave me --
>   Please don't --

Then she tenses, as we HEAR the now familiar SOUND of the Mummy dragging his lame foot behind him, from outside.

>   ANANKA
>   Listen, do you hear?

CONTINUED

198   CONTINUED

The Doctor immediately goes to the door, CAMERA TRUCKS BACK TO A MED. SHOT - TAKING IN THE ENTRANCE DOOR, as he opens it, we HEAR the approaching SOUND of the Mummy increase. The Doctor looks out, then seems to back away, and as he does, we suddenly HEAR a crash and the glass door opposite, that leads to the infirmary, falls to pieces as the Mummy ENTERS through this door....The girl, frightened, backs toward the door to which the Doctor had gone. The Doctor whirls around to face the Mummy. Protectively, he stands between the girl and the Mummy. Before he can escape, the Mummy reaches out and grabs him.

199   EXT. CONSTRUCTION CAMP - <u>NIGHT</u> - MED. SHOT

at the Infirmary. Ananka, dressed in her white robe, RUNS OUT of the office, disappearing toward the swamp...The Mummy comes out and glancing about, lumbers away in another direction.

                                                    FADE OUT

FADE IN

200   INT. WALSH'S ENGINEERING OFFICE - <u>DAY</u> - CLOSEUP OF HEADLINES OF THE BAYOU TIMES

        "MYSTERY SWAMP KILLINGS BAFFLE POLICE"

CAMERA DOLLIES BACK from newspaper to a MED. SHOT ON WALSH at desk. He gets up, and begins pacing the floor in one of his customary, apoplectic moods, swinging the newspaper in his hand...Betty is seated at her desk, typing. In the midst of this action, we HEAR a familiar VOICE o.s.

                    HALSEY'S VOICE
            You wish to see me?

Betty stops her typing to look up. Walsh stops in his tracks to look around, and flings his newspaper aside, as Halsey WALKS INTO SCENE.

                    WALSH
                (takes one look)
            Not with any pleasure, young man...   } OMIT

                    BETTY
                (appealing to Walsh)
            Please...Uncle Pat...

                    HALSEY
                (amused)
            That's frank...if not cordial...

                                                    CONTINUED

200   CONTINUED

> Walsh goes right up to Halsey, CAMERA TRUCKS IN TO A CLOSE TWO SHOT OF HALSEY AND WALSH, losing Betty for a moment.

>>WALSH
>>You know Dr. Cooper was killed...
>>>(challengingly)
>>What have you got to say about it?

>>HALSEY
>>I regret is deeply...but I can't
>>see why you should challenge me...
>>I didn't kill him...

>>WALSH
>>Even since you started monkeying
>>around down here, there's been nothing
>>but trouble....First Antoine...then
>>Tante Berthe the Cafe woman...

> Before Walsh can continue:

>>HALSEY
>>I didn't kill them either...The same
>>mold marks that were found on Tante
>>Berthe's throat -- were found on
>>Dr. Cooper -- The Mummy, Kharis --

> During this dialogue, CAMERA TRUCKS BACK TAKING IN BETTY, who is listening eagerly to the conversation, hoping that Halsey will only keep quiet and not argue with her irascible uncle, who keeps pacing up and down, while she looks to Halsey trying to get his eye.

>>WALSH
>>>(interrupting)
>>Sure -- the Mummy! It's bad enough
>>trying to do something with a lot of
>>ignorant natives...but by Jupiter,
>>you're not going to drive the rest of
>>them away with your Mummy killings...

>>HALSEY
>>>(simply)
>>You could help me catch the Mummy...

>>WALSH
>>>(cutting in - explosively)
>>I'll help you like I'll help you find
>>the missing girl! Just listen to this...
>>>(turns to Betty)
>>I want you to send a telegram to head-
>>quarters...I insist the rights and license
>>granted to Scripps Museam to excavate these
>>swamps be revoked and rescinded at once....

201   GROUP SHOT - HALSEY - WALSH - BETTY

> HALSEY
> Just a minute, Mr. Walsh....

Before he can finish Betty cuts in.

> BETTY
> Now look Uncle Pat...You can't do that...

> WALSH
> Can't I...You just send that wire....
> (firmly; almost yelling at her)
> Do as I tell you...Send it...

> BETTY
> (calmly - quietly but with equal firmness)
> No, Uncle Pat...It's unfair and I won't....

> WALSH
> You won't, huh?
> (looks daggers at Halsey)
> Where's the phone?...I'll send it myself...
> (to Halsey on the cross)
> Good day to you, Dr. Halsey...
> That's all I wanted to say...

Walsh walks OUT OF SCENE.

> HALSEY
> (turns in his direction)
> But that isn't all I have to say to you, Mr. Walsh...

> BETTY
> Please, Jim....

Jim hesitates a moment, then he and Betty turn and cross to the door, CAMERA PANNING WITH THEM.

> HALSEY
> That girl must be somewhere in this vicinity -- and I'm going to find her if I have to search every foot of the bayou myself.

CONTINUED

201 CONTINUED

> BETTY
> (thoughtfully)
> Talk to Big Joe. He knows all
> the trails -- He'll help you.

Halsey nods and both EXIT.

DISSOLVE

202 EXT. SWAMP - <u>NIGHT</u> - MED. SHOT ON A LIGHTED TORCH

moving through the swamplands. The torch moves closer to the CAMERA, and we see that it is being carried by Big Joe who is making his way through the spooky swampland, glancing about. He EXITS FROM SCENE.

203 MED. FULL SHOT - ON BIG JOE

as he moves into the clearing in the swamp, where Halsey is waiting, also carrying a torch. As Big Joe halts near Halsey, Ismail and Abbas come INTO SCENE from another direction, lighted torches in their hands. CAMERA DOLLIES IN TO A MED. CLOSE SHOT ON GROUP.

> HALSEY
> (wearily)
> Don't look like we're having much success.

> BIG JOE
> I fin' that poor girl, sure 'nough.
> I know dem swamp lak my finger.

> ISMAIL
> (quietly)
> Personally, I think the search is hopeless.

> ABBAS
> I do too.

> HALSEY
> (grimly)
> Well, I don't. We'll start out in
> different directions again and meet
> back at the camp. If we don't find
> her tonight, we'll continue searching
> tomorrow.

Ismail and Abbas exchange glances and all EXIT OUT OF SCENE in different directions.

204   MED. FULL SHOT - OVERLAPPING ACTION IN ABOVE SCENE

The four men with torches start into the swamp in different directions. Big Joe crosses to a dugout in the water at the edge of the swamp, and propping his torch up in the bow, gets in and pulls his way on down the boyou.

DISSOLVE

{Dialogue Missing in scenes}

205   EXT. SWAMP - CLOSE MOVING SHOT - <u>NIGHT</u> - ON BIG JOE

poling the swamp water in a dugout. With a smile of confidence on his face, he is a colorful, romantic figure as he stands, tall and unafraid, making his way through these serie surroundings.

     BIG JOE
    (waving to someone
     o.s. and calling to them)
 Wait...wait...

206   LONG SHOT

SHOWING the girl flitting through the dark primeval swampland like a disembodied spirit...

207   CLOSE MOVING SHOT - ON BIG JOE

seeing the girl, starts to pole faster, and as he does the CAMERA PANS FROM HIM TO THE SWAMPLAND BEHIND HIM, CATCHING IN A MED. LONG SHOT THE MENACING FORM OF THE MUMMY, approaching.

208   MED. SHOT - CENTERING ON A HUGE OLD SWAMP ASH OR CYPRESS TREE, BIG AND WIDE AROUND LIKE AN OLD GIANT REDWOOD -

as Ananka breathlessly RUNS INTO THE SCENE, and looking back, sees herself pursued by Big Joe o.s., she climbs around and hides behind the trunk of this tree. She has hardly concealed herself, when Big Joe poles his way INTO SCENE, nosing his dugout right in amidst the roots of the tree, while he scans in every direction for a sight of the girl. He can't figure it out.

     BIG JOE
    (scratching his head)
 That'sa funny....

He puts the pole across his dugout and looks to see what gives around the tree trunk...He thus has his back to CAMERA, still standing in the dugout when suddenly some unseen force, evidently of great power, has grabbed the end of the dugout and starts tipping it up. As the front of the boat is tipped, Big Joe, thrown off balance, falls back OUT OF SCENE, until the dugout stands straight up in almost a right angle to the CAMERA. At the same time we HEAR from o.s. behind CAMERA, Joe's stifled heart-rending CRY.

209   MED. SHOT - FROM A WIDE ANGLE

Ananka, on the other side of the tree trunk, seeing what has happened, starts to RUN and splash away as fast as she can, in the opposite direction.

210   MED. SHOT - AT FOOT OF TREE

We SEE the Mummy crushing the life out of the o.s. Big Joe, in the stern of his dugout. From the distance we HEAR:

> HALSEY'S VOICE (o.s.)
> (calling)
> Joe... Big Joe! ..... } Not Said!

re-echoing through the swampland.

The Mummy paying no attention to the call, and with scarcely a glance at his victim, continues to make his way through the swamps in the direction in which the girl has taken.

211   MED. FULL SHOT - ON ANANKA   *Scene changed to Page 73*

She runs frantically away from CAMERA into swampland. She glances fearfully back; then, as she disappears, a menacing figure of the Mummy lumbers through and EXITS through SCENE after her. Then, we HEAR Halsey's VOICE again, CALLING from o.s., this time closer:

> HALSEY'S VOICE
> Joe -- where are you? — Not Said!

CAMERA SWINGS OVER to PICK UP Jim Halsey making his way through swampland, a lighted torch in his hand. He reaches foreground and glancing about suddenly sees Joe's body o.s.

212   MED. SHOT - FROM HALSEY'S ANGLE

on the lifeless body of Joe, huddled in a grotesque position in the stern of his dugout, the pole floating beside him. The light from Halsey's torch floods the SCENE, then Halsey ENTERS and hurries to dugout where he props up the torch and begins examining Big Joe.

213   CLOSE SHOT - ON HALSEY

examining Big Joe's body o.s. by the flickering light of the torch. He reaches down and feels of Big Joe's throat, then picks up a small piece of tattered wrapping from the Mummy which he holds up, his eyes widening understandingly. He puts the wrapping in his pocket; then, picking up an old blanket from the bottom of the dugout, starts putting it over Big Joe.

214   MED. SHOT OVERLAPPING ACTION OF ABOVE SCENE

Halsey finishes covering Big Joe's body with the blanket; then, putting the torch in the bow of the dugout, he picks up the pole and, getting into the boat starts poling through the swamp in the general direction of the camp.

DISSOLVE

215   EXT. CONSTRUCTION CAMP - NIGHT - MED. FULL SHOT - FROM ELEVATION - ON CAMP ★-Scene begins here!

which is in darkness with the exception of a light in Betty's tent.

216   INT. BETTY'S TENT - NIGHT - MED. SHOT - ON BETTY

seated in a chair near her cot, attempting to read a book. A lantern is hanging from a tent-pole above her head. She puts the book down and gets nervously to her feet. CAMERA DOLLIES IN as she glances at a clock which shows the hour of two. Then the SOUND of o.s. FOOTSTEPS is HEARD, and she whirls and hurries across to tent flap, CAMERA PANNING WITH HER. She starts to untie the flap, as Ananka's VOICE is HEARD outside.

                ANANKA'S VOICE
                  (calling)
        Miss Walsh -- Miss Walsh.

217   EXT. CONSTRUCTION CAMP - NIGHT - MED. CLOSE SHOT - IN FRONT OF BETTY'S TENT

Betty unties flap, and steps out as Ananka hurries breathlessly INTO SCENE.

                ANANKA
        May I stay here with you?
                  (looks toward the
                  light on the
                  tentpole inside)
        Where there's light. I'm so afraid
        of the night -- and the darkness.

                BETTY
                  (worried)
        But Dr. Halsey and the others --
        They're looking for you.

                ANANKA
                  (ignoring this)
        Please let me stay in the tent
        with you.

As Betty nods a dubious agreement, Ananka ENTERS the tent. Betty hesitates a moment, then follows, closing the tent flap after her. We SEE silhouetted figure begin tying the flap.

218   EXT. EDGE OF CONSTRUCTION CAMP - NIGHT - MED. FULL SHOT - ON THE MUMMY

as it COMES INTO SCENE from among the trees and halting near Abbas' tent in foreground, continues on OUT OF SCENE, in direction of Betty's tent. As he disappears, Abbas' tent flap opens and Abbas stealthily appears. He edges back in the shadows to watch.

219   INT. BETTY'S TENT - NIGHT - MED. CLOSE SHOT - ON BETTY

as she finishes tying the tent flap, then turns and crosses to Ananka, CAMERA PANNING WITH HER. Ananka stands underneath the lantern, a pathetic, distraught looking creature.

> BETTY
> Why did you run away after Dr. Cooper was killed -- and why are you afraid of the darkness?

> ANANKA
> (pathetically)
> I don't know.
> (then pleadingly)
> If you'd only help me find myself.

Ananka sits down on the cot, huddled like a frightened animal, CAMERA DOLLIES IN TO CLOSE SHOT.

> ANANKA (cont'd)
> I remember being brought here to this tent -- and I was very happy. Then -- he came to take me away.

220   CLOSE SHOT - ON BETTY

She stares toward Ananka in amazement.

> BETTY
> Who -- who came to take you away?

Following dialogue not used.

221   MED. CLOSE SHOT - ON ANANKA

as Betty steps INTO SCENE with her.

> ANANKA
> (emotionally)
> The High Priest of Karnak.
> (almost whispering)
> Three thousand years ago I died -- a cursed death.

Betty stares toward Ananka in frightened wonderment.

CONTINUED

bk   75

221   CONTINUED

                        ANANKA (cont'd)
            He said -- I am the reincarnated spirit
            of the Princess Ananka. Now he has   } Not Used.
            come to take me back -- to Kharis --

                        BETTY
                     (suddenly understanding)
            Kharis -- the mummy?

      Ananka jumps to her feet, clinging to Betty's arms.

                        ANANKA
            But it's not true -- I'm not --

      Ananka's words are halted by the sudden SOUND of the tent
      tearing and both whirl in terror.

222   MED. CLOSE SHOT - REVERSE ANGLE - ON KHARIS

      the Mummy as he finishes tearing the side of the tent and
      steps inside.

223   MED. SHOT - ON TENT INT. - OVERLAPPING ACTION OF ABOVE
      SCENE

      as the Mummy moves forward toward the two girls, Betty lets
      out a horrified gasp, but Ananka, with a little moan, col-
      lapses on the cot. The Mummy moves on toward Ananka, and
      as Betty turns to run, he pushes her aside with such
      force that she falls to the tent floor, dazed. CAMERA
      DOLLIES INTO CLOSE SHOT as the Mummy picks up the inert
      body of Ananka and turning, heads back across the tent.
      He strikes the tent-pole with his dragging leg, and as he
      crashes on OUT, through the torn flap, the tent collapses,
      the lantern going out.

224   EXT. CONSTRUCTION CAMP - MED. FULL SHOT - ON BETTY'S TENT-
      OVERLAPPING ACTION OF ABOVE SCENE

      The tent collapses and the lantern goes out. The Mummy
      is still carrying the limp figure of Ananka, turns and heads
      out into the swampland. CAMERA PANS WITH HIM as he dis-
      appears from sight.

225   MED. SHOT - ON ABBAS -

      in the shadows of the trees near his tent. His eyes follow
      the Mummy and Ananka, then he glances about and hurries
      across in the direction of Betty's tent, CAMERA PANNING
      WITH HIM.

226 MED. SHOT - ON BETTY'S COLLAPSES TENT.

We see the folds of the tent move as the dazed Betty inside tries to free herself. Then Abbas runs INTO SCENE. As he starts to help the girl get out, Goobie rushes fearfully IN and halts near Abbas, frightened and amazed.

> GOOBIE
> Has sumpin' done happened to Miss Betty?

> ABBAS
> (still working)
> Help me loosen this tent, and we'll find out, Goobie.

[handwritten: Goobie Not included here nore this scene]

Goobie helps Abbas with the canvas, and soon Betty is uncovered and Abbas helps her to her feet.

227 MED. CLOSE SHOT - ON THE THREE

> BETTY
> (frightened)
> We must find Dr. Halsey, Abbas. The Mummy --
> (glancing off)
> The Mummy took the girl away.

> GOOBIE
> (terrified)
> The Mummy?

> ABBAS
> (feigned amazement)
> What girl?

> BETTY
> That strange girl you were looking for. She came to my tent -- then the Mummy broke in -- and carried her away.
> (then pleadingly)
> You were searching the swamp with Dr. Halsey. You've got to help me locate him.

228 CLOSEUP - ON ABBAS

as he looks toward Betty, o.s., and we see an odd gleam come into his cold eyes.

> ABBAS
> He's not far from here, Miss Walsh. I'll guide you --

F:

229 MED. CLOSE SHOT - ON ABBAS, BETTY AND GOOBIE

                    BETTY
                (relieved)
        Thank you, Abbas.
                (then to Goobie)
        I'll be back before long, Goobie.
        Don't say anything to alarm my uncle. } Not Said!

Goobie nods in open-mouthed awe and shakes his head as Betty turns and follows Abbas away from the camp, CAMERA PANNING WITH THEM.

230 MED. FULL SHOT - ON ABBAS AND BETTY

as they hurry away from camp and plunge into the swamplands in general direction of that taken by the Mummy and Ananka.

231 EXT. SWAMP - NIGHT - MED. PAN SHOT ON THE MUMMY

carrying the limp Ananka, moving through the swamp in the direction of the Monastery.

232 MED. FULL SHOT - ON ABBAS AND BETTY

as they hurry into scene from b.g. and make their way swiftly along a winding trail through the swamps.

233 EXT. SWAMP LANDING NEAR CAMP - NIGHT - MED. SHOT - ON HALSEY

as he pulls dugout up to landing in swamp. Big Joe's blanket-covered body is SEEN in the boat and the torch is still blazing in the bow. Halsey steps ashore; then, taking a torch glances grimly down on Big Joe's blanket-covered figure. Then, turning, he EXITS from scene toward camp proper, CAMERA PANNING WITH HIM.

234 EXT. CONSTRUCTION CAMP - NIGHT - MED. FULL SHOT - ON HALSEY

as he hurries into camp, carrying the torch. He halts in amazement as CAMERA PANS HIM INTO SCENE with Betty's wrecked tent, where Gooby is trying to straighten it out. He turns and hurries in that direction.

235 MED. CLOSE SHOT - ON GOOBIE

trying to straighten the tent. He whirls as Halsey comes into SCENE carrying the lighted torch.

                                        CONTINUED

235   CONTINUED

> GOOBIE
> (amazed)
> Massah Halsey - de's jes gone lookin' fo' yo'!
>
> HALSEY
> What are you talking about, Goobie? Who's looking for me -- and where is Miss Walsh?

[margin note: Goobie is confronted but is not aware of Betty's disappearance nor of what has happened.]

> GOOBIE
> (excitedly)
> Dat's wha' I's tryin' t' 'splain! Dem feller, Abbas -- take de boss' niece up do ol' road into de swamps to fin' yo' after she say de Mummy wreck' de tent and carry 'way de odder girl!!

[margin note: Dialogue not used.]

Halsey reacts in grim understanding to this.

> HALSEY
> (grimly)
> I'm going after them. Wake up Walsh and tell him to follow... Betty's probably in great danger!

[margin note: ✱ Begin correct scene here.]

Without waiting for Goobie to reply, Halsey turns and hurries away from camp in the direction taken by Abbas and the girl. CAMERA PANS WITH HIM.

236   MED. FULL SHOT - ON HALSEY

as he dashes to the edge of the camp and lighting his way with the torch, turns and starts out toward the old road to the trees and through the old swamp land.

237   MED. FULL SHOT - ON GOOBIE

as he watches Halsey disappear; then, wailing, runs frantically back toward Walsh's tent, CAMERA PANNING WITH HIM as he halts in front of tent and calls:

> GOOBIE
> (fearfully)
> Massah Walsh! -- Massah Walsh!! GET UP! .... de Mummy's on de loose an' he's dancin' wit' de debbil!!!

Walsh is SEEN to come out of the tent-flap, slipping into a robe while a few other workmen come from their tents, ad libbing excitedly.

DISSOLVE

F:
Goobie dialogue not used!

238   EXT. SWAMP - NIGHT - MED. SHOT

as the Mummy, still carrying Anaka in his arms, makes his way in the dark, between tree stumps and moss hangings.

239   MED. FULL SHOT - ON ABBAS AND BETTY

hurrying along trail through swamp land.

240   MED. SHOT - ON HALSEY

as he comes into scene carrying the torch. Then, halting in f.g. he glances about at the ground.

241   CLOSE SHOT - DOWN ANGLE - ON IMPRINT OF MUMMY'S GOOD FOOT AND DRAGGING LEG IN THE SOFT CLAY

CAMERA PANS OVER to pick up the imprints of Betty's foot and Abbas' shoes. All prints lead in the same direction.

242   MED. CLOSE SHOT - ON HALSEY

as he realizes he's on the right trail and moves grimly on into the swamps CAMERA PANNING WITH HIM.

243   MED. FULL SHOT - ON WALSH, GOOBIE, ACHILLES AND A COUPLE OF OTHER WORKMEN

all carrying torches and rifles, hurrying along the road through the swamps. They halt to pick up the trail, then move on, CAMERA PANNING WITH THEM.

                                                         DISSOLVE

* Scene changes to page 83

244   INT. CEREMONIAL ROOM - NIGHT - MED. FULL SHOT

as Ismail, dressed in his Priestly robes, stands between the two mummy cases, as though in last minute inspection. The cases are on the floor ready for their destined occupants.

Following omitted from film!

                    ISMAIL
                (calling o.s.)
        Abbas!

He pushes both Mummy cases a little further apart and makes his way toward the CAMERA as if surprised that his call is not answered.

                    ISMAIL
                (in sterner fashion)
        Abbas!!

                                                        CONTINUED

F: OMITTED! 80

244 CONTINUED

Again receiving no reply, he looks off greatly surprised. As he crosses the Ceremonial Room, he stops to look into the brazier, turns it over, and finds it is empty. He kneels to get box, finds tana leaves and puts them on to brew. As CAMERA DOLLIES into MED. CLOSE SHOT.

          ISMAIL (cont'd)
         (greatly upset)
Abbas!!!

Receiving no response, he starts hurrying OUT toward door which leads toward the Monk's wing, CAMERA PANS WITH HIM AND HOLDS ON THE HEAVY DOOR as he EXITS FROM SCENE.... As it holds, we suddenly HEAR from the opposite direction the familiar dragging SOUND of someone APPROACHING, CAMERA PANS OVER TO THE OPPOSITE SIDE, picks up the Mummy coming in from the main entrance, still holding the girl, Anaka in his arms.

245 MED. CLOSE SHOT - ON MUMMY HOLDING THE LIMP FORM OF ANAKA

as he places her in one of the cases, he looks about as if seeking the High Priest Ismail, but neither the High Priest nor his disciple Abbas are there. He stands looking down upon this girl who, still mortal and alive, can not become his bride until she has been mummified like himself. Like a helpless automaton, he looks about, not knowing what to do without his mentor, the High Priest. He leans over the girl.

246 CLOSE SHOT - ON ANAKA - SHOOTING DOWN UPON HER

The Mummy, leaning over her INTO THE PICTURE. Slowly she opens her eyes and then weakly whispers:

          ANAKA
Kharis... I am tired...
    (wearily)
Take me with you... so that
I may know... rest....

She closes her eyes again, as though in sleep. CAMERA TRUCKS BACK STILL TILTED DOWN, as Kharis pulls himself up to his full height and looking around starts searching frantically for Ismail. CAMERA PANS him out a side door.

F: 81

247   EXT. PATH NEAR MONASTERY - <u>NIGHT</u> - MED. SHOT - ON ABBAS
       AND BETTY

   as they hurry along the path and up to Monastery steps,
   CAMERA PANNING WITH THEM. Abbas starts up and Betty
   glances about her somewhat uneasily.

248   MED. CLOSE SHOT - ON THE TWO

                    BETTY
                  (uneasily)
       Why should Dr. Halsey be waiting *(dialogue used)*
       here ---- in this old ruin?

                    ABBAS
                  (with dignity)
       If you wish to turn back ----

   Betty eyes the calm Abbas for a moment, then shakes her
   head, and turning starts up steps.

   Abbas conceals his satisfaction and walks up the steps
   with Betty. CAMERA PANS WITH THEM.

249   EXT. SWAMP - <u>NIGHT</u> - MED. SHOT - ON HALSEY

   moving hurriedly along through the swamp, carrying a
   torch. He notices a path leading through a wooded section
   and turning, EXITS in that direction.

250   MED. FULL SHOT - ON WALSH, GOOBIE, ACHILLES AND
       THREE WORKMEN

   hurrying along through swamps with their rifles and torches.
   They pick up the Mummy's trail and head on in that direction.

ec (scenes changed and omitted for entire page!)

251 EXT. MONASTERY ENTRANCE - NIGHT - MED. FULL SHOT - ON MUMMY

as he comes out of the monastery apparently still looking for Ismail. He glances about, then makes his way around corner of building.

252 EXT. PATH NEAR MONASTERY STEPS - MED. FULL SHOT - ON HALSEY

as he hurries in from b.g. and CAMERA PANS WITH HIM up to the steps where he halts in amazement and glances about. Then, as he glances up the steps, his eyes widen.

253 LONG SHOT - REVERSE ANGLE - SHOOTING UP MONASTERY STEPS

showing Abbas and Betty disappearing from view.

254 MED. CLOSE SHOT - ON HALSEY

as he takes out his revolver and makes sure it is in working condition, then puts out the torch and hurries up the steps.

255 INT. CEREMONIAL ROOM - NIGHT - MED. FULL SHOT

as the door opens and Abbas ENTERS with the still uneasy Betty. He leads the way across the room and Betty halts in amazement as she sees the two mummy cases, ceremonial paraphenalia and the brazier to brew the tana leaves. She glances toward the now smugly smiling Abbas, and she steps to the mummy cases, and slowly her eyes go to the form of Ananka inside. CAMERA DOLLIES slowly in to a MED. CLOSE SHOT on Betty and Abbas. Betty stares down in amazement at Ananka in the mummy case.

256 MED. CLOSE SHOT - HER ANGLE - ON ANANKA

Apparently in the state of trance in the mummy case, her long hair around her beautiful face.

257 MED. CLOSE SHOT - ON BETTY AND ABBAS

Slowly Betty glances up towards Abbas, and her eyes widen understandingly.

                    BETTY
                  (awed)
        Now I understand why she said she
        died three thousand years ago. She's --
        she's Princess Ananka --
                    CONTINUED

257   CONTINUED

Scene begins here from page 79.

                    ABBAS
                (quietly)
        The bride of Kharis...
                (then glancing down
                 on Ananka in the case)
        ...In a fraction of life's moment
        Ismail will lift her mortal state --
        she will be sealed in this case --
        and, with Kharis, sent to Egypt,
        there to be embraced by the sands
        of the past!

                    BETTY
                (amazed)
        Ismail?

                    ABBAS
        Yes!...The High Priest of Karnak.
        I am his humble assistant.

                    BETTY
                (glancing somewhat
                 fearfully about)
        ...Where is Dr. Halsey? You told
        me he was here.

                    ABBAS
                (suggestively)
        This monastery has been abandoned for
        nearly 100 years. Dr. Halsey has no
        idea of its existence.

Betty's eyes widen at Abbas' words; as Abbas moves toward her and she recoils. Both halt at Ismail's calm voice o.s.

                    ISMAIL'S VOICE
        You have nothing to fear, Miss Walsh.

258   MED. SHOT - ON ISMAIL

standing inside the back doorway of the Ceremonial Room. His eyes gleam contemptuously as he moves across to Abbas and the frightened Betty, CAMERA PANNING WITH HIM.

                    ISMAIL
                (to Betty)
        You will be allowed to return to the camp --
        on your promise to keep silent about what
        you have seen here!

                                        CONTINUED

258   CONTINUED

Then he confronts Abbas menacingly.

> ISMAIL
> The Curse of Amon-Ra upon you, Abbas!
> (then, stepping closer)
> Your tongue shall be torn from your mouth -- for the vows you have sworn to -- falsely!

During this dialogue CAMERA DOLLIES IN to a CLOSE THREE SHOT.

> ABBAS
> (somewhat fearfully)
> I am but flesh and blood -- I do not believe --

— Dialogue missing

> ISMAIL
> (interrupting)
> Vultures shall pick the flesh from your bones -- after Kharis learns of your treachery!!

Ismail emphasizes his words by turning and picking up a handful of tana leaves, and dropping them into the steaming brazier. Betty watches fascinated, as Abbas moves menacingly forward.

> ABBAS
> (menacingly)
> I, too, know the secret of the tana leaves, Ismail -- without the brew Kharis is powerless.

259   CLOSE SHOT - ON ABBAS OVERLAPPING DIALOGUE OF ABOVE SCENE

As he finishes speaking, he suddenly pulls a dagger and plunges it down, o.s., apparently into the throat of Ismail, who lets out an unworldly shriek which ends in a gasp and is followed by the dull thud of a fallen body. Betty's horrified SCREAM dies in her throat, o.s., as CAMERA TRUCKS QUICKLY BACK TO MED. SHOT ON ABBAS, THE FALLEN BODY OF ISMAIL AND THE TERRIFIED GIRL. Abbas looks contemptuously down at the body, then throwing the dagger to one side, steps to the brazier, CAMERA PANNING WITH HIM as he crosses, KEEPING IN BETTY, but X-ING OUT the body of Ismail.

CONTINUED

259   CONTINUED

Abbas reaches out to tip the brew over but the sound of a door closing o.s. startles him and he whirls. CAMERA SWINGS SWIFTLY OVER to the front door on Monastery and we SEE Halsey COMING IN, gun in hand. He moves warily forward o.s. toward Betty and Abbas.

260   MED. SHOT - ON BETTY AND ABBAS

The body of Ismail on the floor behind the table is partly concealed. Halsey steps into scene, gun in hand and glancing down at the body of Ismail moves forward to confront Abbas as Betty runs to him.

> BETTY
> (brokenly)
> Jim -- please take me away from here -- this is all so horrible!

CAMERA DOLLIES IN to CLOSE SHOT ON THE THREE.

> ABBAS
> (cringing, as though afraid)
> Master - - I meant no harm - -

As Abbas is speaking, his hand reaches behind him and clutches a metal torch and, suddenly swinging around, lashes out with it and knocks the gun from Halsey's hand. Halsey is overbalanced and sprawls backward out of scene. *Abbas never releases knife and uses it instead of torch.*

261   MED. SHOT OVERLAPPING ACTION OF ABOVE SCENE

as Halsey falls backward. Abbas, still holding on to the metal torch, springs forward and tries to knock Halsey out with it. *Halsey never is struck or knocked down. It is Abbas who is temporarily knocked out loosing knife*

262   CLOSE SHOT - ON HALSEY

Halsey pulls away but cannot completely side-step out of the way.

263   CLOSE SHOT - ON TORCH

as it hits Halsey, with back to CAMERA, on the side of face, neck and shoulder, knocking him OUT OF PICTURE with the blow. → *NOT DONE!*

264   MED. CLOSE SHOT - ON GIRL

as she SCREAMS AND BACKS OUT OF SCENE.

265   CLOSE SHOT - ON ABBAS

trying to follow up his advantage, takes another swing.

266   CLOSE SHOT - ON HALSEY - REVERSE ANGLE

as he ducks and comes into a clinch, forcing Abbas back, almost throwing him INTO CAMERA. We see Halsey's face and neck scratched and bleeding. - Not done ↑

267   CLOSE SHOT - ON ABBAS - SHOOTING OVER HALSEY'S SHOULDER

Halsey hits Abbas with an upper-cut that snaps the Egyptian's head right back on his shoulders...

268   MED. SHOT - ON HALSEY AND ABBAS - GIRL SUGGESTED COWERING IN B.G.

Halsey following up the punch closes in again on Abbas. In and out the props, around the room, the two men go at it hammer and tongs, in life and death struggle.

269   EXT. PATH NEAR MONASTERY STEPS - NIGHT - MED. SHOT - ON WALSH, ACHILLES, GOOBIE AND THREE WORKMEN

making their way along path.

270   INT. CEREMONIAL ROOM - NIGHT - MOVING SHOT OF ABBAS

Abbas never letting go of the metal torch, hangs onto it, brandishing and threatening this lethal weapon like a heavy-weight nursing his Sunday punch, as he weaves in and out, waiting for opening. He lets go a vicious swing with it.

271   CLOSE SHOT - ON HALSEY

just ducking under it. The torch lands on his arm, causing it to go limp with the blow. THE CAMERA, A LITTLE MORE CAUTIOUS NOW, STAYS AT A RESPECTABLE DISTANCE, FOLLOWING THE FIGHT IN AND OUT AROUND THE ROOM. NOW PICKING UP THE GIRL - NOW LOSING HER, as shrinkingly, she tries to hide around the Mummy cases...

272   CLOSE TWO SHOT - HALSEY AND ABBAS

Halsey succeeds in getting in close for in-fighting and thus avoids the Mary-Ann with the lethal torch...

273   MED. SHOT - FIGHT - HALSEY'S ARM

comes up with a terrific uppercut to catch Abbas right on the button, knocking him back OUT OF SCENE, Halsey lunging after him.

274   EXT. MONASTERY STEPS - NIGHT - MED. FULL SHOT - ON WALSH GOOBIE, ACHILLES AND THREE WORKMEN

as they reach steps and start up.

275   INT. CEREMONIAL ROOM - NIGHT - MED. SHOT

as Halsey lunges forward to finish the fracas, one arm limp at his side, he stumbles and trips to fall on his knees. Before he can get up, Abbas seizing his advantage is right on him like a vicious beast, with the metal torch upraised. *All fight scenes changed as Halsey always gets the better of things.*

276   CLOSE SHOT - ON ABBAS

with metal torch upraised, we see him fiendishly bring it down with all the energy left in him. We HEAR an o.s. crashing blow, presumably on Halsey's skull. *→ Changed. Abby's awakes after being knocked out and attempts to knock out Halsey with torch but Khavis, entering, destroys the attempt*

277   MED. SHOT - HALSEY, ABBAS

Halsey falls flat OUT OF PICTURE, with Abbas towering over him. CAMERA SWINGS OVER to a door where we see the Mummy come IN.

278   MED. CLOSE SHOT - ON THE MUMMY

as he moves on into room, CAMERA PANNING WITH HIM. He halts at table where brew is steaming and sees the partly concealed body of Ismail on the floor. He becomes almost human in his grief, and then picking up the hot steaming brazier, drinks all of its contents, and as he drops the heavy utensil to the floor, CAMERA DOLLIES IN, TAKING IN Abbas, the terrified Betty and Halsey sprawled on the floor Abbas, who is moving toward Betty, halts at the sound of the brazier dropping. Then, as the girl runs to Halsey's side, Abbas whirls and tries to escape from the enraged Mummy who moves toward him. *Not Done.*

279   MED. CLOSE SHOT - FROM LOW ANGLE - ON HALSEY AND BETTY

as Halsey begins to come to. Abbas is seen backing into b.g., the Mummy following him.

280   MED. PAN SHOT - ON ABBAS AND THE MUMMY

as the Mummy reaches out to grab Abbas, Abbas whirls and dashes into a smaller room, slamming the barred door after him.

281   INT. MONK'S CELL - NIGHT - MED. CLOSE SHOT - ON ABBAS - ANGLE SHOT OUT THROUGH BARS TOWARD MUMMY

Abbas slams the door, locking the cell. Then the Mummy enraged at finding himself locked out, grabs hold of the bars on the door and begins pulling them from their masonry. As a few stones fall down around them, Abbas begins begging for his life.

>   ABBAS
> No -- Do not harm me, Kharis. If you
> destroy me -- the secret of the tana
> leaves will die --

Abbas' words halt as the Mummy, with the last powerful yank, gets the door loose and plunges into the cell. The dust and masonry start falling around him.

282   MED. CLOSE SHOT - ON ABBAS

as he backs to the other wall. The Mummy looms INTO SCENE, PAST CAMERA and grabs Abbas by the throat. Abbas screams. Then as he drops from the Mummy's clutches, terrific crash SOUNDS and other masonry and rocks pour down upon the Mummy from above.

283   INT. CEREMONIAL ROOM - NIGHT - MED. FULL SHOT - SHOOTING PAST HALSEY AND BETTY

who get to their feet, staring toward door into Monk's room. With another terrific crash, masonry and rocks pour down into Monk's cell and the surplus rolls out into the Ceremonial room, blacking the door.

284   EXT. MONASTERY - NIGHT - MED. SHOT - ON WALSH, ACHILLES GOOBIE AND THREE WORKMEN

as they halt at the SOUND of the Monk's cell collapsing from inside. Then, as the last rumbling sound dies away, Walsh leads the way and all hurry into the Monastery.

sm   89

285   INT. CEREMONIAL ROOM - NIGHT - MED. FULL SHOT - ON ROOM

Halsey and Betty stand in center of the room, near the partly concealed body of Ismail and the two mummy cases. The dust is settling from the now blocked and shattered door into the Monk's cell. Walsh, Achilles, Goobie and the three workmen hurry in and as they cross to Halsey and the girl who turn to see them, CAMERA DOLLIES IN TO MED CLOSE SHOT ON GROUP.

>   WALSH
>   What in the world has been happening
>   up here, Halsey?
>
>   HALSEY
>   (nodding toward
>   Monk's cell)
>   The Monk's wing collapsed, burying
>   the Mummy and Abbas.
>
>   WALSH
>   Then you and Betty are all right?

As Halsey nods, his arm tightens around Betty. Walsh glances down toward Ismail, o.s.

* - Goobie finds Ananka's casket and yells for others to come and see it

>   WALSH
>   (perplexed)
>   Who's this?

286   CLOSE SHOT - ON WALSH, BETTY AND HALSEY

>   HALSEY
>   That is Dr. Ismail Farouk -- my   → Not Said!
>   trusted assistant who happened to
>   be the High Priest intent on
>   stealing the Mummies.
>   (then to Betty)
>   Where's the girl -- Ananka?

Betty, without a word, turns and crosses to the mummy cases followed by Halsey and Walsh. CAMERA PANS WITH THEM, and they halt at the cases. They glance down inside and Halsey exclaims in amazement:

>   HALSEY
>   Look -- here.

As all glance down at the case and their eyes widen,

                                                          CUT TO

sm *Halsey explains how Ananka had reverted to her mummy state — But Walsh still does not Believe a word of it.*

287   CLOSE SHOT - ON PRINCESS ANANKA IN THE MUMMY CASE

She has gone through a metamorphosis and has returned to the mummy state of an old decrepit hag.

288   MED. CLOSE SHOT - ON GROUP

around Mummy case. Halsey steps forward and puts the lid on the case and then turns to the others.

> HALSEY
> (with a sign of relief)
> I never thought I'd get her...   — Not Said
> (then with genuine admiration)
> And in such beautiful condition...

> WALSH
> I never would have believed it...   — Not Said
> if I hadn't seen it with my own eyes....

Halsey closes the lid of the Mummy case. CAMERA HOLDS ON WALSH, as he shakes his head in bewilderment.

289   CLOSE SHOT - ON MUMMY CASE

as Halsey finishes fastening it...CAMERA PANS TO THE OTHER MUMMY CASE, standing beside it empty, we HEAR:

> HALSEY (o.s.)
> Now all we've got to do is put a
> crew of men to work digging Kharis
> out of the rubble and cart them
> both down to camp.

CAMERA PANS OVER TO TAKE IN HALSEY AND BETTY, as he puts his arm around her and starts walking with her toward entrance door.

> HALSEY
> (smiling at Betty)
> Well, the Scripps Museam should
> be satisfied....

> BETTY
> (smiling back)
> And I hope you will be too...

> HALSEY
> (noncommittal)
> In a way, yes.....

Betty looks up him.

CONTINUED

289   CONTINUED

                    HALSEY (cont'd)
            After we're married...I'd like
            to do some work in Yucatan...

                    BETTY
                    (suspiciously)
            More Mummies?

                    HALSEY
            Oh no...Hidden Temples...

                    BETTY
            And do they kill people in them?...

                    HALSEY
                    (smiling at her)
            No...The ancient Mayans enjoyed a
            highly cultured civilization.

    The rest is lost...as they walk PAST CAMERA.

                                        WIPE TO

— all dialogue completely omitted and changed.

290   EXT. MONASTERY STEPS - NIGHT - MED. FULL SHOT

    fascinatingly highlighted by the last rays of the fading
    moon. Halsey, Betty, and party ENTER SCENE and start
    down the Temple steps, CAMERA PANS WITH THEM

                                        FADE OUT

    ↑ *Correct End!*

            "THE END"

Halsey & Betty speak of hinted marriage and Walsh agrees explaining that Betty is no good as a secretary after falling for Halsey.

PRESSBOOK SECTION

The Mummy's Curse

with

PETER COE
KAY HARDING
MARTIN KOSLECK
VIRGINIA CHRISTINE
KURT KATCH

UNIVERSAL

PUBLICITY

"The Mummy's Curse," Universal's newest thrill-film, stars Lon Chaney as the Mummy, and features Peter Coe (right) in the role of a high priest; their unfortunate victim is lovely Virginia Christine.

THE MUMMY'S CURSE (2A)

New 'Mummy' Film Stars Lon Chaney

(Advance)

From the numerous horror roles Lon Chaney portrays, one could easily form the idea that the actor lives in a cob-web covered castle, dines on a stew of bats' wings, and walks in his sleep. On the contrary, motion pictures' No. 1 quiver star has about as sane an off-screen existence as anyone in Hollywood. Chaney, for example, upon finishing his latest thriller, Universal's "The Mummy's Curse," which is due .... at the .... Theatre, left for his 1300-acre ranch in Northern California to do the fall plowing.

During shooting of the picture, laid in a moss-strewn swamp in Louisiana, the actor would end the day by unwrapping the yards and yards of mummy bandages from his body, removing the gruesome greasepaint from his face and hands, and going home—to feed his chickens and turkeys.

Chaney lives on a small "residence-ranch," as they are known in the San Fernando Valley. Only a few acres, it is still large enough for fruit trees, fowl and a couple of horses, and is within B-card distance of Universal City.

The "Mummy" stories have proved one of Chaney's most popular horror groups. "The Mummy's Curse" is the fifth of the series, and features Peter Coe, Kay Harding, Martin Kosleck, Virginia Christine, Dennis Moore, Leslie Goodwins directed; Oliver Drake produced.

THE MUMMY'S CURSE (1A)
Lon Chaney is seen as the terrifying Mummy in Universal's thriller, "The Mummy's Curse." Others in the film are Peter Coe, Kay Harding, Martin Kosleck, Virginia Christine. Leslie Goodwins directed.

Dennis Moore Active Actor

(Current)

Winners of the Purple Heart, who happen also to be friends of Dennis Moore, have received carved figures, of a Purple Heart done in African natural colored hardwood from the actor.

Moore has already presented four of the figures, which are much prized by the recipients. He is prepared to make as many as required to honor his friends wounded in service, though each carving takes considerable time to prepare.

Moore devoted spare moments to his hobby between scenes of Universal's "The Mummy's Curse," horror drama, now at the .... Theatre, in which he plays a romantic lead opposite Kay Harding, in support of Lon Chaney.

The actor, who is almost a one-man "hobby lobby," also collects pipes. He has 265 kinds, resting in a rack he carved himself. He "saves" harmonicas, too, having one model that cost as much as a grand piano—$500.

Moore is very proud of his skill at grafting roses. One of his bushes has 14 varieties of blooms. If and when he should get bored with the above hobbies, the actor turns to painting pictures or meeting with members of his motorcycle club.

THE CAST

Mummy	Lon Chaney
Ilzor	Peter Coe
Princess Ananka	Virginia Christine
Betty	Kay Harding
Halsey	Dennis Moore
Ragheb	Martin Kosleck
Cajun Joe	Kurt Katch
Pat Walsh	Addison Richards
Dr. Cooper	Holmes Herbert
Achilles	Charles Stevens
Sacristan	William Farnum
Goobie	Napoleon Simpson

CREDITS

Universal Pictures Presents
LON CHANEY
in
"THE MUMMY'S CURSE"
with
Peter Coe - Kay Harding
Martin Kosleck - Virginia Christine
Kurt Katch - Dennis Moore
Addison Richards

Screen Play by Bernard Schubert; Original Story and Adaptation by Leon Abrams; Dwight V. Babcock; Director of Photography, Virgil Miller, A.S.C.; Musical Director: Paul Sawtell; Art Direction: John B. Goodman, Martin Obzina; Director of Sound: Bernard B. Brown, Technician: Robert Pritchard; Set Decorations: Russell A. Gausman, Victor A. Gangelin; Film Editor: Fred R. Feitshans, Jr.; Music and Lyrics by Oliver Drake and Frank Orth; Special Photography by John P. Fulton, A.S.C.

Directed by .... Leslie Goodwins
Assoc. Producer. Oliver Drake
A UNIVERSAL PICTURE

SYNOPSIS

(Not for Publication)

Draining of a bayou swamp area is halted when superstitious Cajun workmen learn one of their number has been mysteriously murdered. The men whisper fantastic tales about mummies being buried in the area.

Walsh (Addison Richards), boss on the job, is annoyed at their fear and further angered when Dr. James Halsey (Dennis Moore) of the Scripps Museum, and his associate, Dr. Ilzor Zandaab (Peter Coe), arrive to search for the mummies of Kharis (Lon Chaney) and Princess Ananka (Virginia Christine), believed buried in the swamp. Walsh refuses to cooperate, ridiculing the mummy idea, although his pretty niece and secretary, Betty (Kay Harding) shows interest both in the story and in Halsey.

Bulldozers unknowingly uncover the mummies, and that night Dr. Zandaab secretly meets Ragheb (Martin Kosleck), a workman, who takes the scientist to a hidden monastery. There the mummy, Kharis, lies in a sarcophagus. It is revealed that Zandaab is actually an Egyptian priest and Ragheb his servant. Zandaab revives Kharis with a brew of Tana leaves, and Kharis goes in search of his beloved Princess Ananka, whom the sun has transformed into a beautiful young girl.

Ananka fears Kharis and hides in the construction camp. Three people are murdered by Kharis before he catches her. Zandaab is then destroyed by a workman, and Kharis dies in ruins of the collapsed monastery, as Ananka returns to her ancient mummy state.

'Mummy's Curse' Thrill-Laden Film

(Review)

Another of Universal's popular and exciting "Mummy" pictures arrived yesterday at the .... Theatre. It is "The Mummy's Curse," starring Lon Chaney and featuring in support Peter Coe, Kay Harding, Martin Kosleck, Virginia Christine, Kurt Katch, Dennis Moore and Addison Richards. "The Mummy's Curse," even more thrilling than its predecessors, tells the suspenseful tale of mummies Kharis and Princess Ananka, unearthed by bulldozers during the draining of some bayou swamp country. Kharis is revived by High Priest Peter Coe with a brew of Tana leaves. The Princess, played by Virginia Christine, is restored to youth and beauty by the warmth of the sun.

She fears Kharis and escapes him, hiding in the construction camp. Three people are killed by Kharis before he catches her, and is himself destroyed.

Lon Chaney in the role of Kharis is frightening enough to satisfy the most thrill-hungry film fans. Virginia Christine does an excellent job as the Egyptian Princess, and Kay Harding and Dennis Moore, who try to protect her from the Mummy, are fine, too.

The film was directed by Leslie Goodwins under the associate producership of Oliver Drake.

This is the fifth of the "Mummy" pictures, all of them dealing with the adventures of Kharis, the Mummy, and his beloved Princess Ananka.

Gets Old Fast

(Current)

The remarkable "aging" jobs done by make up men recently on Barbara Stanwyck, Bette Davis, Alexis Smith and other actresses, would still leave them looking like young girls alongside Virginia Christine in Universal's "The Mummy's Curse," which is now at the .... Theatre.

Miss Christine "ages" 5000 years in one jump—from a beautiful maid to a living mummy princess of Egypt. The actress, wife of Fritz Feld, appears in support of Lon Chaney, who is starred as the Mummy. The role is her biggest so far, and for it Virginia had to hide her lovely blonde hair under an Egyptian-looking black-haired wig.

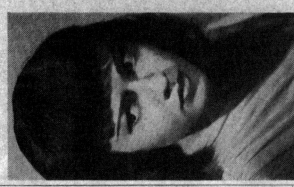

THE MUMMY'S CURSE (1C)

Virginia Christine portrays Princess Ananka, quest of the Mummy's search, in Universal's chiller, "The Mummy's Curse." Lon Chaney is seen as the Mummy.

Screen Nazis Change Types

(Advance)

A sign that Nazis are approaching their end on the screen, too, is the appearance of two such Nazi-typed actors as Martin Kosleck and Kurt Katch in non-goose-stepping roles in Universal's thriller, "The Mummy's Curse," which comes .... to the .... Theatre.

Kosleck plays an Egyptian in the horror picture, and Katch a Cajun native of Louisiana.

Both actors rose rapidly to screen fame through their adroit portrayals of Nazi villains. Kosleck was cast in nothing but German roles until recently, while the majority of Katch's assignments were as swastika-ites.

Lon Chaney is starred in "The Mummy's Curse," and is supported in addition to Kosleck and Katch by Peter Coe, Kay Harding, Virginia Christine and Dennis Moore.

The film tells the story of the return to life of the Egyptian mummies, Kharis, and Princess Ananka. As Mummy, Lon Chaney commits a number of murders before he succeeds in returning the Princess to her original mummy state.

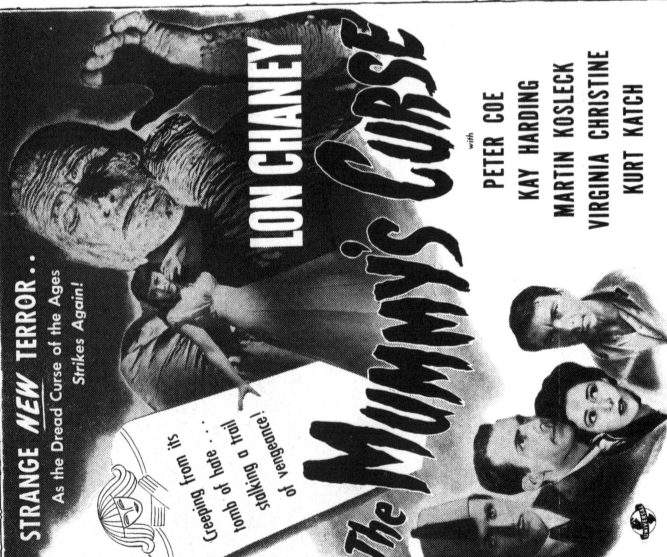

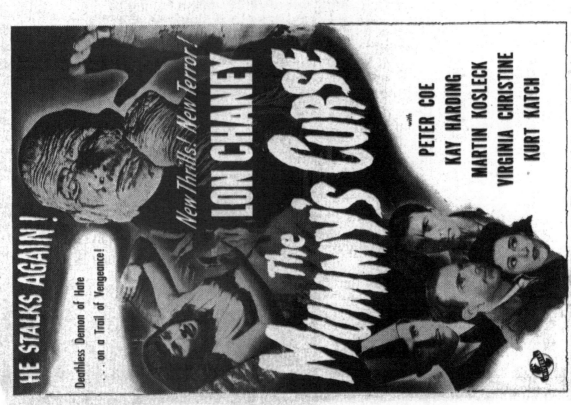

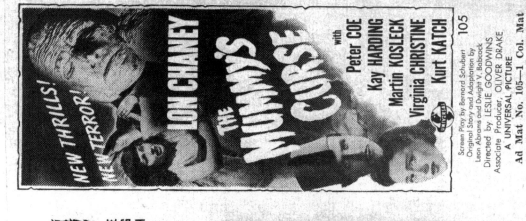

Virginia Christine A Barefoot Actress

(Current)

How long does it take to become a barefoot boy—or girl—again?

Not as long as you might guess. Virginia Christine became a barefoot girl in one week, hardening the soles of her feet sufficiently so she could walk on almost any kind of ground without undue discomfort.

Miss Christine toughened her soles in order to go barefoot in "The Mummy's Curse," in which she portrays an Egyptian mummy, living and beautiful. The Universal thriller is now at the .... Theatre.

Through scene after scene the actress walks dreamily amid tangled jungles and down rocky paths. The only time she rests her feet in a scene is when her fellow-mummy, Lon Chaney, carries her.

Miss Christine hails from the corn country, and when a child, went without shoes all summer.

She hardened her feet by walking barefoot around her house and yard for two days. Then she climbed a dirt trail in the Hollywood hills near her home, going a little farther up the mountain each day.

Also daily the actress bathed her feet in hot vinegar—copying a trick used by prizefighters who soak their hands in vinegar to harden them.

THE MUMMY'S CURSE (1B)

An exciting moment in Universal's new horror film, "The Mummy's Curse." Lon Chaney is starred as the Mummy; Kay Harding is the girl in danger.

Home Towns

Lon Chaney .. Oklahoma City, Okla.
Peter Coe .. Dubrovnik, Jugo-Slavia
Kay Harding .. Cushing, Oklahoma
Martin Kosleck .. Pomerania, Germany
Virginia Christine .. Stanton, Iowa
Kurt Katch .. Grodno, Poland
Dennis Moore .. Fort Worth, Tex.
Addison Richards .. Zanesville, Ohio

Universal Thriller Features Peter Coe

(Current)

Good-looking Peter Coe, who had just gotten started on his screen career when he enlisted in the Marine Corps, is back in circulation in the cinema city, following his recent honorable discharge from the service. Prior to the departure of Universal's Jugoslav star for war duty, however, he had finished the role of High Priest in that studio's new thriller, "The Mummy's Curse," starring Lon Chaney, and currently at the ...... Theatre. Coe portrays the Egyptian official who restores Kharis, the Mummy, to life, with a brew of Tana leaves.

Coe, who made his film debut in "Gung Ho!" and followed that with appearances in "Gypsy Wildcat" opposite Maria Montez, and "House of Frankenstein," is a recruit from the stage. His work in the Broadway version of "My Sister Eileen" called him to the attention of film scouts, and netted him a contract with Universal.

He Works at It

(Current)

Lon Chaney, who suffers more for his art than anyone in Hollywood, dropped seventeen pounds in the confining mask and costume of the Mummy which he wears in his current Universal thriller, "The Mummy's Curse."

The film, now at the .... Theatre, stars Chaney and features Peter Coe, Kay Harding, Martin Kosleck and Virginia Christine.

This wasn't Chaney's first experience in the wrappings of the Mummy, having appeared in the role several times.

SHOWMANSHIP

NOVEL LOBBY BOARD

You can arouse a lot of curiosity, and create plenty of enthusiasm about "THE MUMMY'S CURSE" by having your sign shop build a giant lobby board decorated with Egyptian design. Fill it with scientific questions, pertaining to ancient Egyptian mysteries such as . . .

HOW CAN A MUMMY BE KEPT ALIVE FOR 3000 YEARS?
IF BULLETS WON'T KILL A MUMMY . . . WHAT WILL?
ARE THE ARCHEOLOGISTS WHO OPEN A MUMMY'S TOMB . . . DOOMED?
WHAT WAS THE SECRET OF KHARSIS THE SECOND?
WHO WAS THE MONSTER THAT WOULD NOT DIE?
HOW DID THE ANCIENT EGYPTIANS PRESERVE THEIR DEAD?

Then follow up on these questions with this one lettered in bigger and bolder type . . . WILL YOUR NERVES STAND THE THRILL OF "THE MUMMY'S CURSE"? SEE IT HERE STARTING FRIDAY!

SELL IT ON THE AIR

Ancient Egyptian mystery legends fascinate all imaginative people. Capitalize on their curiosity by using spot announcements on the radio after mystery and horror air shows.

RADIO ANNOUNCEMENTS

STATION BREAKS . . . 3000 years of terror . . . breaking loose! All new thrills as the most dreaded curse of the ages strikes again! See Lon Chaney as Kharis the mummy in "THE MUMMY'S CURSE."

Strange new terror! Strange new thrills! The mummy is creeping from its tomb of hate . . . stalking a trail of terrible vengeance! See Lon Chaney as "The Monster That Would Not Die" in "THE MUMMY'S CURSE."

FIFTY WORD ANNOUNCEMENT . . . "THE MUMMY'S CURSE" All New Thrills! All New Horrors! . . . As the dread terror of an ancient curse stalks from the depths of doom! Can a mummy be kept alive for 3000 years? Will your nerves stand the thrill of "THE MUMMY'S CURSE" ? ? ? SEE Lon Chaney—the screen's master of menace in "THE MUMMY'S CURSE."

USE POSTER CUT-OUTS

The excellent poster material on "THE MUMMY'S CURSE" is ideal for making effective lobby displays. The three and six sheets are particularly well suited for eye-stopping standees and "sock" lobby set pieces. Mount on strong beaver board with strips of wood for extra reinforced backing. Cut out around the Mummy's head and also around the figure of the girl.

STREET BALLY

Here's an eye-stopping ballyhoo that should arouse a lot of comment. Have your sign shop build a Sarcophagus or a mummy, such as described below, embellished with Egyptian decoration, which your poster artist can scare up in his files. (See illustration.)

Have a truck or horse drawn vehicle carry following copy lettered on banners attached to the sides of the wagon . . . "WE HAVE CAPTURED THE MUMMY . . . IS HE DEAD OR ALIVE? DOES HE CARRY A CURSE?" SEE HIM AT THE RIVOLI NOW!

MUMMY LOBBY DISPLAY

You can make up a mummy for lobby display by using a clothing store window dummy. Fold arms across chest and tie in place. Wind two inch gauze or strips of cloth around the body. Cover face with mud pack which you can buy at a cosmetic counter. Wind cloth over head, chin and across forehead. Leave face unbandaged.

Spray with grey paint, and while still wet throw fine ashes over entire figure. When dry brush off excess ash dust. Use a sign with this copy . . . THE DREAD TERROR OF AN ANCIENT CURSE STALKS FROM THE DEPTHS OF DOOM! SEE "THE MUMMY'S CURSE" STARRING LON CHANEY . . . HERE FRIDAY!

POSTERS

ONE SHEET

Order All ACCESSORIES From Your LOCAL NATIONAL SCREEN SERVICE EXCHANGE

SIX SHEET

LOBBIES

EIGHT 11x14s

14 x 36

22x28

MIDGET WINDOW CARD

REGULAR WINDOW CARD

THREE SHEET

Printed in U.S.A.

MagicImage Filmbooks presents
The Phantom of the Opera
(1925)

INCLUDES:
Complete Production History from those who were there!
The Complete Press Book!
The Complete Shooting Script
Rare Behind the Scenes Photographs
Contributions by
Mary Philbin ("Christine"),
Cinematographer Charles Van Enger,
Ron Chaney and MORE!

**320 Pages!
over 250 photos!
$24.95**

Order On-Line at *www.magicimage.com*

Shipping
$ 5.00 first book
$ 3.00 each additional
$ 8.00 per book Canada
$15.00 per book Overseas

MagicImage Filmbooks
740 S. Sixth Avenue,
Absecon, NJ 08201
Phone: (609) 652-6500
Fax: (609) 748-9776
www.magicimage.com
sales@magicimage.com

"A real treat for any diehard movie buff or scholar...brimming with wonderful information and hard to find material."

-Leonard Maltin,
"Entertainment Tonight"

MagicImage Filmbooks

Endorsed by Chaney Enterprises

ORDER VIA THE WEB, FAX, MAIL OR PHONE!!

Reissued! LONDON AFTER MIDNIGHT

THE reconstruction that started it all! *MagicImage*'s most popular book ever is being re-issued after being out of print for 15 years. Now you can experience the MOST FAMOUS LOST FILM of all time-- Lon Chaney's 1927 horror classic *London After Midnight*. See the entire film reconstructed from original studio stills and publicity shots. Experience this lost classic for only $24.95 + shipping.

DON'T MISS IT THIS TIME AROUND!
ORDER TODAY!

The London After Midnight Multimedia Experience

See it roll across your computer screen! Includes an original music score accompaniment by MagicImage composer John Conforti!

CD-ROM $15.95

Also Coming ONLY from *MagicImage*!

Order On-Line at *www.magicimage.com*

Shipping
$ 5.00 first book
$ 3.00 each additional
$ 8.00 per book Canada
$15.00 per book Overseas

MagicImage Filmbooks
740 S. Sixth Avenue,
Absecon, NJ 08201
Phone: (609) 652-6500
Fax: (609) 748-9776
www.magicimage.com
sales@magicimage.com

ORDER VIA THE WEB, FAX, MAIL OR PHONE!!

Abbott & Costello
BUCK PRIVATES

The Definitive History of Bud & Lou's First Film!

By Ronald Palumbo
As GI's marched off to fight WWII, Bud and Lou marched over the silver screens on the home front with this screwball comedy. Read the original script and the complete, authoritative production history by one of the foremost experts on the films of Abbot & Costello. Order your copy today for only $19.95 + shipping.

Order On-Line at *www.magicimage.com*

Shipping
$ 5.00 first book
$ 3.00 each additional
$ 8.00 per book Canada
$15.00 per book Overseas

MagicImage Filmbooks
740 S. Sixth Avenue,
Absecon, NJ 08201
Phone: (609) 652-6500
Fax: (609) 748-9776
www.magicimage.com
sales@magicimage.com

MagicImage Filmbooks

Also available...
Abbott & Costello
  Meet Frankenstein
Dracula
The Wolf Man
and many more....

ORDER VIA THE WEB, FAX, MAIL OR PHONE!!